Becoming an SAP™ Consultant

Your Guide to Professional and Financial Success

Send Us Your Comments:

To comment on this book or any other PRIMA TECH title, visit our reader response page on the Web at **www.prima-tech.com/comments**.

How to Order:

For information on quantity discounts, contact the publisher: Prima Publishing, P.O. Box 1260BK, Rocklin, CA 95677-1260; (916) 632-4400. On your letterhead, include information concerning the intended use of the books and the number of books you wish to purchase. For individual orders, visit PRIMA TECH's Web site at **www.prima-tech.com**.

Becoming an **SAP**™ Consultant

Your Guide to Professional and Financial Success

Gareth M. de Bruyn

Ken Kroes

SERIES EDITOR:
Robert Lyfareff

A Division of Prima Publishing

A Division of Prima Publishing

Prima Publishing and colophon are registered trademarks of Prima Communications, Inc. PRIMA TECH is a trademark of Prima Communications, Inc., Rocklin, California 95677.

"SAP" is a registered trademark of SAP Aktiengesellschaft, Systems, Applications and Products in Data Processing, Neurottstrasse 16, 69190 Walldorf, Germany. The publisher gratefully acknowledges SAP's kind permission to use its trademark in this publication. SAP AG is not the publisher of this book and is not responsible for it under any aspect of press law.

R/2, R/3, SAP Business Workflow, ABAP/4, SAP EarlyWatch, SAP ArchiveLink, R/3 Retail, SAPPHIRE, SAP Solution, and ALE/WEB are either trademarks or registered trademarks of SAP Aktiengesellschaft, Walldorf, Germany.

Windows, Windows Explorer, and Microsoft are registered trademarks of Microsoft Corporation.

Prima Publishing and the authors have attempted throughout this book to distinguish proprietary trademarks from descriptive terms by following the capitalization style used by the manufacturers.

ISBN: 0-7615-1884-3
Library of Congress Catalog Card Number: 98-67706
Printed in the United States of America

99 00 01 02 03 HH 10 9 8 7 6 5 4 3 2 1

Publisher:
Stacy L. Hiquet

Associate Publisher:
Nancy Stevenson

Managing Editor:
Dan J. Foster

Sr. Acquisitions Editor:
Deborah F. Abshier

Project Editor:
Kevin W. Ferns

Editorial Assistant:
Brian Thomasson

Copy Editor:
Richard Adin

Technical Reviewer:
Jon Reed

Interior Layout:
Marian Hartsough

Cover Design:
Prima Design Team

Indexer:
Sharon Hilgenberg

To my family. Please share this accomplishment with me.
You inspire me to reach for new heights.

To G2 Solutions for allowing me the time
to invest in this publication.

Finally, to all of you who said it could not be done.

— GMd

To my wife Donna
and my children, Megan and Jarid,
thanks for your support for the past several months.
Thanks to Rene Massinon,
who taught me so much during my first years
in the consulting industry.

— KK

Acknowledgments

To Matt Carleson, our publisher, thanks for your continued support and vision in the process of writing this book and in the entire series. To Debbie Abshier, thanks for your patience and moral support throughout the writing process. We wish to thank Kevin Ferns for the excellent editorial work on this book. Thank you Jon Reed and Robert Lyfareff for your insightful and valuable comments about the work in progress. Thank you to Robert Parkinson, Clifton S. Thomas, and Pat Breland for answers to technical questions in this process.

Finally, we wish to thank SAP America.

About the Authors

GARETH M. DE BRUYN is an independent SAP consultant and a technical lead for a Fortune 50 company. With many years of experience in the IT industry and over four years in the growing SAP arena, he is a veteran of multiple SAP implementations and most modules of R/3. He can be contacted at gmdebruyn@bigfoot.com.

KEN KROES specializes in implementing SAP for clients with build-to-order (configurable) products and Internet applications for SAP. He has over 15 years of programming and consulting experience and has worked as an independent SAP consultant in both R/2 and R/3 for many large clients. He can be contacted at kenkroes@bigfoot.com.

About the Series Editors

GARETH M. DE BRUYN'S background includes chemical engineering, UNIX site administration, and network installations. A native of South Africa but raised and educated in the United States, de Bruyn believes SAP technology is revolutionizing international business. He plans to earn a law degree to unite his technical and international business skills to capitalize on this global opportunity.

ROBERT LYFAREFF is a veteran of several successful SAP installation teams over the past four years. Coupled with his formal training in computer science and electrical engineering, this unique SAP experience enables him to write about real-world business situations and issues. What excites and challenges him about his work is the integration and modification of business practices with the new technology. Currently, he works as an independent SAP consultant and author.

Contents at a Glance

Contents

Foreword

In the not-so-distant past, becoming an SAP consultant was almost as easy as taking an SAP training course and hanging up a shingle. There seemed to be no rules. The money was so good that *Computerworld* ran a cartoon comparing the SAP consultant to the professional athlete.

But times have changed. On the positive side, SAP is so institutionalized in the Fortune 100 that you can now speak realistically about a career in SAP. But for those trying to break into the field, as well as those already consulting, the rules of the game are starting to take shape: rigorous technical screening, competition for open positions, and increased emphasis on the right kind of experience and certification.

To succeed in this new SAP environment, we need to assemble the the right tools. One major piece of the toolbox is the right information. In *Becoming an SAP Consultant*, two experienced SAP consultants, Gareth de Bruyn and Ken Kroes, provide us with their insight into the SAP consulting field. Using this book, the experienced SAP consultant will be able to hone in on the pieces of the puzzle they still don't have. Those who have not entered the SAP consulting field will find the mystique of the SAP consultant broken down into understandable pieces—pieces that can be added to an existing skill set.

As someone who has worked with SAP professionals for many years, I've seen how many have avoided SAP consulting in favor of the stability of the established company. *Going independent* is a major lifestyle adjustment. You're essentially running a business-of-one—and running this business means you have to secure your own client base, negotiate your own rates, and even handle your own retirement plan decisions. The best thing about *Becoming an SAP Consultant* is that it gives you the entire picture, right down to the nitty gritty of personal finance, which is something SAP consultants, just like professional athletes, cannot afford to ignore. Everything you need to know to run your own SAP career can be found somewhere in this book, from the how-to's of SAP certification to handling your exit from the client site, from managing expenses and per diems to surviving technical interviews.

When you are making decisions about your SAP career, you need to understand the range of options ahead of you and choose the right one with confidence. The big money in SAP is, for the most part, reserved for those who have the fortitude and skill to go out on their own and claim their place in the market. With the information in this book, you can plan for that transition if it suits you. If you are simply looking for more information on breaking into the SAP field, you'll find that here too. This book will work for you on the level you are ready for. And the principles of success on client engagements will have value even beyond an SAP-focused career. After all, aren't the technical careers of the 90s ultimately project-focused? And couldn't we all use a book that directly addresses this type of career, and speaks to us with an authority and attention to detail that only an experienced consultant could provide?

The SAP marketplace will continue to bewilder and challenge even the most experienced consultants. Appropriately enough, the concluding reference sections of this book serve as checkpoints that we can turn back to frequently to get our bearings. The authors' comments on new technical directions in SAP round out the book nicely. We can feel certain that if we follow the same principles that are presented herein, we might also be able to make SAP less of a short-term preoccupation and more like a career choice—one at the center of IT-business change. It makes sense that the independent SAP consultants, the ones with the expertise to pick and choose the best projects, will find themselves at the center of these important changes in global business. Would it not be ideal, then, to hear from some of these consultants, if only they were willing to impart the secrets of their trade?

My thanks to both authors for writing this book and doing exactly that.

Jon Reed
Author, *Opportunities in SAP* newsletter
Allen Davis & Associates

Introduction

Welcome to the incredible world of SAP consulting. This will be your guidebook and shining light to becoming an effective consultant. It takes years to hone all the skills you'll most likely need, but this book will help you achieve that goal by starting you off on the right track or helping you to improve those skills if you are a veteran consultant.

Who Should Read this Book?

This book was written with the SAP professional, specifically the SAP consultant, in mind. But whether you're a technical ABAPer, a business process analyst, a project manager, or other ERP consultant, you'll find what you're looking for to improve your business and professional success.

What This Book Covers

Part I, "Starting Out in SAP," covers getting started with SAP consulting, from résumés to interviews to financial planning. Part II, "The SAP Work Environment," covers the issues you will deal with once you arrive at the client site. Finally, Part III, "SAP Architecture," covers the types of SAP work available and the architecture behind most SAP implementations. These three parts are divided into the following chapters:

Chapter 1, "SAP Today," details the history of SAP and where its future lies. It also outlines some of the new and exciting SAP technologies. Chapter 2, "Résumés," deals with creating an effective SAP consultant's résumé. Chapter 3, "Interviews," covers how to market yourself in an interview. Chapter 4, "Agents," shows you how to pick an agent and make the most out of your relationship. Chapter 5, "Contracts," explains the finer points of negotiating and getting what you need to protect yourself. Chapter 6, "Working Abroad," covers the topic of SAP work outside of the US, including converting money and planning for culture shock. Chapter 7, "Streamlining Operations," shows you how to organize your personal life and make more time for yourself when you're not working. Chapter 8, "Financial Planning," offers some tips and wisdom for investing and saving.

The first chapter of Part II is Chapter 9, "Your First Week," which details your strategy for making stellar first impressions and understanding the dynamics of the people you work with. Chapter 10, "Your Last Week," maps out your gameplan for leaving on the right foot. Chapter 11, "Workplace Etiquette," outlines the traits of a professional and highly-respected consultant. Chapter 12, "SAP Documentation," covers documentation found in SAP as well as how to provide adequate documentation for your client. Chapter 13, "SAP Certification," discusses the pros and cons of certification. Chapter 14, "Training," details the means and methods of gaining valuable training in the dynamic SAP market.

At the beginning of Part III, Chapter 15, "New Implementations," introduces you to the setting of a project when you're starting out. Chapter 16, "Upgrades," tells you how to deal with the goings on of an upgrade project in R/3. Chapter 17, "Support," covers supporting solutions remotely, both while you're on the project and after you finish your contract. This chapter introduces you to some effective tactics to handle support issues. Chapter 18, "Design," is a reference chapter, discussing the overall technical and design considerations of an R/3 implementation.

Conventions Used in This Book

To comfortably absorb the information this book presents, you should be familiar with the teaching tools you'll find throughout. You'll see some special typographical devices to call your attention to certain points in the text:

 TIP

Tips present helpful information in an attention-getting format. They reinforce key concepts and explanations, making them easier to remember and use.

 NOTE

Notes provide additional related information, alternatives, or commentary that might help you better understand the topic under discussion or lead you to additional sources of information.

CAUTION

Cautions warn of potential hazards and pitfalls you should be aware of.

These conventions will serve as your signposts throughout this text. Use them to help you identify critical elements and information about SAP.

Contacting the Authors

We hope that this book helps you to become a better consultant, and we welcome all comments and questions. Please feel free to contact us via e-mail with any questions or comments.

Gareth M. de Bruyn, gmdebruyn@bigfoot.com

Ken Kroes, kenkroes@bigfoot.com

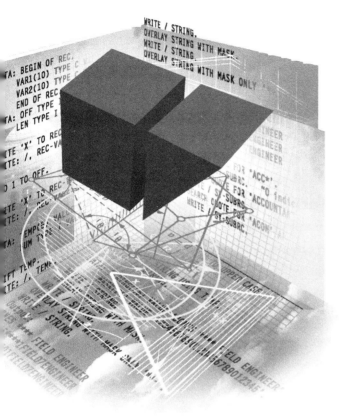

PART I

Starting Out in SAP

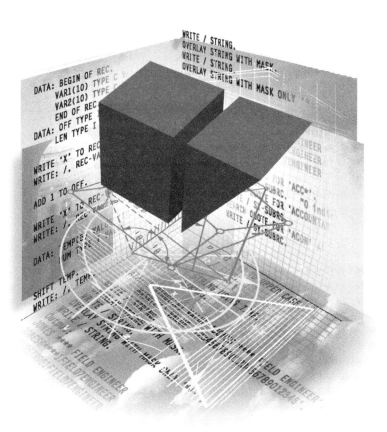

Chapter 1

SAP Today

Several years ago, the experts said the market was saturated, that too many people were getting into the information technology (IT) area, and that rates would be coming down soon. This has not been the case. The millennium is almost upon us, and the demand for good SAP consultants is stronger than ever. In this chapter, we explain why the demand has not decreased and why we expect it to stay this way for the foreseeable future. We also discuss some of the new and exciting areas that SAP and the Enterprise Resource Planning (ERP) software area in general are starting to branch into, and what a consultant should be doing now to prepare for them.

The IT Consulting World

The current high demand for skilled IT professionals is not limited to the SAP area. Some studies indicate that there will be a need for 40 percent more software engineers worldwide within two years. Consider the following:

- ◆ In the next decade, the U.S. Department of Labor projects another 1.3 million workers will be needed to fill new high-tech jobs.
- ◆ "The demand for people who can develop and use the tools of the modern age has vastly outstripped the existing supply," according to *The New York Times* ("Software Jobs Go Begging, Threatening Technology Boom," Jan. 13, 1998).
- ◆ *The Wall Street Journal* notes that "because of those empty desks, companies are cutting back programming projects, delaying new products and trimming expansion plans" ("Filling High-Tech Jobs is Getting Very Tough," Dec. 1, 1997).

Even skills in older technologies such as COBOL are in high demand. The year 2000 issue and the introduction of the Euro in Europe are the two most significant factors driving this demand for older technology skills, as many companies do not want to install brand new solutions, but simply fix their existing systems.

There is a continuous demand for skilled people in the new technologies of object-oriented programming, Internet/intranet Web development, and SAP and other ERP solutions as well. Consider the explosive growth of the Internet and the speed at which technology evolves in this area. Companies are scrambling to keep up to date with the latest version of HTML (hypertext markup language), e-commerce, security, JAVA, and other new innovations, which takes up a significant portion of the total IT resource pool. There is also the entire ERP industry and the reengineering of processes and intrabusiness communication, as well as the integration of solutions.

There is no conclusive evidence of a major increase in the number of people graduating from colleges and universities with IT backgrounds. Even at the current graduation levels of students with this classroom experience, it takes at least five years of solid industry experience before most people are capable of successfully designing, implementing, and consulting in the IT area.

With the supply and demand situation as it is, there is another trend developing, which is that more IT people are working under contract. Contract work is generally associated with a lack of job security, but as long as work is plentiful, this risk is reduced. The result is that large organizations become accustomed to using contract help, and have difficulty retaining the most sought-after people. There are more jobs available, and if you are well qualified, there are more opportunities for you to land a contract.

SAP and ERP Solutions

As with most technologies today, the leader of the pack has a distinct advantage. The leader becomes a pseudo-standard for the industry, and competitors play catch-up just to keep hold of their market share. In this type of scenario, a competitor must have a better and cheaper product to overtake the leader. In general, companies are unwilling to risk money investing in solutions that may not be around in a few years, so they bet on the leader.

As Table 1-1 illustrates, SAP is by far the leading provider in ERP solutions. The values in the table are from fiscal year 1997. The ratios between the companies for 1998 appear to be even more in SAP's favor.

Table 1-1 1997 Total Sales, ERP Solutions

Company	Billions of Dollars
SAP	3.58
Oracle (Applications Only)	1.80
PeopleSoft	0.82
Baan	0.68

Because SAP is the largest in the business, it also attracts most of the third-party software vendors. Installing SAP is only the beginning of the total data integration within a company. Clients have to purchase third-party software to perform those tasks not supported by ERP software after SAP is installed, and they will want to ensure that they have a wide choice of products to choose from. By going with SAP, they are guaranteed the largest base of third-party software.

As Table 1-2 illustrates, SAP's research and development budget is about equal to that of its next three competitors combined. The research and development money that SAP is investing is going into both improving and expanding its already broad software base. SAP is currently focusing on the smaller business market with aggressive pricing and systems that do not take as much time to set up.

Table 1-2 1997 Research and Development Investments

Company	Millions of Dollars
SAP	482
Oracle	270
PeopleSoft	130
Baan	91

New SAP Modules

SAP is also adding new modules and branching out into new business areas.

SAP SCOPE

The SAP Supply Chain Optimization, Planning, and Execution (SAP SCOPE) initiative provides solutions that integrate information and decisions from the entire supply chain. SCOPE creates a framework for integrating strategic decision support, data warehousing, planning and simulation, optimization, forecasting, sales force automation, and customer relationship systems into one system. In general, SCOPE is divisible into these areas:

- ◆ SAP APO (Advanced Planner and Optimizer) is SAP's module for the advanced supply chain planning, which allows for real-time planning and decision support.
- ◆ SAP's BBP (Business-to-Business Procurement) module allows businesses to have closed-loop procurement, including the use of the Internet.
- ◆ SAP Logistics Execution System (LES) is an enhanced warehouse and transportation management system that performs the physical connection between the APO and BBP supply chain solution.

What makes SCOPE so powerful is its tie to the rest of SAP's core modules such as finance, logistics, and human resources. This is a good example of how SAP leverages from its strengths. Other companies are trying to provide similar solutions to SCOPE, but their products do not integrate as well with the other modules that link an entire company together.

Sales and Service Modules

In the past, SAP concentrated on the basic business areas of finance, human resources, project planning, procurement, and manufacturing. With its sales and service module, SAP plans to penetrate the office side. The sales module supports sales force automation and mobile sales. The service module supports mobile service. SAP plans to release additional modules that support marketing and other aspects of sales over the next few years, and you can expect the sales and service modules to be out sometime later this year.

Workflow

Although Workflow has been around since release 3.0, it is really only now that it is gaining practical use. SAP Business Workflow provides the infrastructure and tools that allow business processes which cross over more than one department to be treated as one process instead of several smaller processes. Workflow is easily integrated into the end user presentation server and interacts with applications such as Microsoft Excel and Outlook. It also provides easy links into the Internet and intranet. There is a wealth of documentation and examples of practical uses for Workflow at SAP's Web site (**www.sap.com**). Read them to become familiar with Workflow's new functionality since release 4.0.

Data Warehousing

A data warehouse is a separate application environment, with a dedicated database that draws on many data sources and supports query and analysis. The Data Warehousing module in SAP (BIW, Business Information Warehouse, or BW) is designed specifically for R/3, but can be integrated into other systems as well. BIW has an integrated OLAP (online analytical processing) engine and contains open BAPIs (business application programming interfaces) for third-party data sources and analytical tools. It comes pre-configured with many commonly used queries, and has an interface called the Business Explorer, which end users can use to build and execute queries. As businesses become more integrated, there is an opportunity for large productivity increases with easy analysis of combined departmental data. There are also opportunities for work for consultants who can clearly demonstrate to a client how this type of information can be of direct benefit.

After the Initial ERP Installation

As many customers discover after installing SAP, it is not the friendliest system for end users, nor is there an immediate gain in productivity. Installing SAP is not the end of the data integration process; it is just the beginning of the evolution to a totally integrated system.

There is usually a decrease in productivity for the first few months after the go-live procedure. This is due to the fact that many people need to learn new job functions and communications with the SAP system. During this initial period, there is usually some tuning required to maximize the software's performance, which can also reduce overall productivity.

After the go-live stage is over, there is usually a period where new processes are introduced to take advantage of the integration the ERP system provides. There is also a tendency during this stage to install add-on software to the ERP system to further enhance the productivity gains. It is during this stage that management in a company must embrace change to truly reap the benefits of the initial installation of the ERP system. SAP R/3 is a solid foundation for such changes, as it centralizes data and support services.

As this reengineering philosophy becomes more apparent to companies, there will be a growing need for more and more development, enhancement, and reengineering in general for existing SAP sites, which means more work for the SAP consultant that can provide knowledgeable, practical solutions to the client's problems.

Market Demand

Certain areas always seem to have a high demand regardless of what the latest trend is. These areas are usually related to fundamental SAP areas such as data archiving and electronic data interfaces.

Data Archiving

Data archiving may seem like a boring area, but the demand for people remains strong. One reason for this is that consultants who know about data archival also know a lot about all of the SAP modules, and this is a fairly rare trait. SAP does provide the tools (such as the transaction SARA), yet they still need to be configured, and bolt-on tables need to be dealt with. Additionally, there are some areas in which SAP has not provided any archiving tools (such as classification systems).

Another archiving problem is integration with a company's data warehouse strategy. Data warehouses run on their own databases, so before data is archived from an SAP system, it must be analyzed to determine whether it should go into the data warehouse (and how it should get there) if it is not already a part of the data warehouse.

Data archival also goes hand-in-hand with the obsolescence of stock and materials for companies. Many corporations have bloated inventories of obsolete parts because they do not have an easy and integrated way of identifying and removing these items from their books. These excess inventories cost companies money, and people that can help reduce this are always in demand.

Electronic Data Interfaces

There has always been a demand for people who can get data transferred from one system to another. With more and more businesses integrating, the role of electronic data interfaces (EDI) will expand over the next few years. In fact, a new Web-based EDI standard, XML, is currently being debated.

Part of what makes EDI a high-demand area is that an EDI consultant has to interface with two different systems. Even though the protocol is the same, the configurations are usually different and translations of the data often need to be done on both sides.

Staying on the Cutting Edge

SAP has introduced object-oriented technology into the R/3 system by making R/3 processes and data available in the form of SAP Business Objects. External applications can access the SAP Business Objects using standardized, platform-independent interfaces (BAPIs). The SAP Business Objects and their BAPIs provide an open, object-oriented view of the business processes and data in an R/3 system. If you are involved in any of the technical areas of SAP, it is important that you keep up with this technology, as it dictates how other software packages and systems interface with SAP. The BAPI interfaces in SAP are currently the cutting edge technology in data manipulation and retrieval techniques, and will soon be the standard method for accessing data.

See SAP's Web site and join its Open BAPI Network (**www.sap.com/products/ techno/bapis/bapi.htm**), as shown in Figure 1-1. From this Web page, you can join the Open BAPI Network and have access to loads of information on BAPIs in general, their implementation in SAP, information on additional training, examples, FAQs, and more.

Another area to pursue is that of programming with JAVA. SAP has announced that it will support the JAVA programming language from within SAP. SAP does not intend to replace Advanced Business Application Programming (ABAP) with JAVA, but SAP will give clients a choice of programming languages to work in. JAVA can also be used in Remote Function Calls (RFC), and you can download the SAP JAVA RFC Class library and documentation from SAP's Web site (**www.sap.com**).

What this means to an SAP ABAP programmer is that if you do not want to limit yourself to ABAP contracts only, you should learn JAVA and understand how it integrates into SAP. Of course, the best way to keep in touch is to read about the newest developments from both SAP and its competitors. This may sound like a

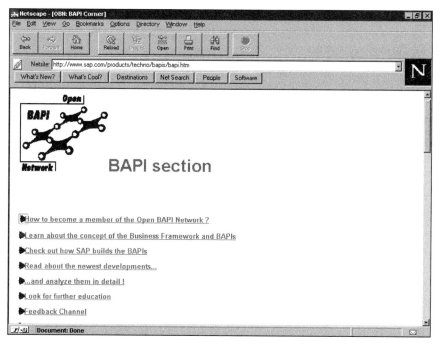

FIGURE 1-1 *SAP's BAPI Web site*

lot of work, but just looking once a month for a few hours on the Internet will keep you informed. Especially useful is the ERPSuperSite (**www.erpsupersite.com/**), which gives a rundown of the ERP industry in general. It keeps important news headlines around for a few months, so viewing this site once a month works well.

SAP and the Internet

Quite a bit of SAP's research and development money has been going to develop an Internet/intranet-friendly product, and we believe that this is where technical consulting is heading over the next several years. SAP's approach to the Internet is threefold.

The first approach is the opening of SAP enterprise applications to Internet solutions through BAPIs: learn BAPIs and JAVA.

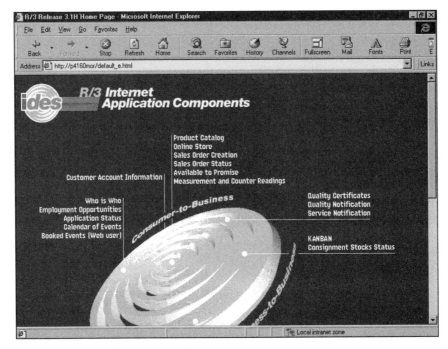

FIGURE 1-2 *SAP's Internet Applications Component Web site*

The second approach to the Internet is SAP's combining of prebuilt components to deliver complete Internet business solutions and business scenarios. SAP offers customers the choice of whether to implement comprehensive Internet business solutions or to implement components individually.

The third approach that SAP is taking is the delivering of prepackaged Internet application components that include intuitive Web interfaces designed for casual users, along with the tools to quickly implement solutions over the Internet (see Figure 1-2).

Internet Transaction Server

The Internet Transaction Server (ITS) allows a company to run standard SAP transactions and reports through its intranet. Though this tool is still fairly limited in scope, it is still a very powerful tool and all consultants should be aware of it. Using a tool such as Web Studio, the developer creates the HTML that is used by the Internet Transaction Server to build the Web page. Once a user brings up one of these pages, the ITS system gets the user's input (mouse click or data field entries), passes this input to SAP through a dialog session, and finally returns the results, all via a Netscape or Internet Explorer browser.

One of the advantages of this system is that users who do not need to log on to SAP for other reasons can simply click on a Web link and get the information they want. There is no need to have them learn the SAP graphical user interface or support additional logons to the SAP system.

The combination of the ITS and Web Studio solution does have drawbacks, however. Currently, simple functions such as F1 for help or F4 for possible choices do not work unless they are specifically programmed. Also, things such as selecting multiple entries via select options do not work.

SAP Employee Self Service

SAP doesn't limit its Internet development to new modules. SAP has developed the Employee Self Service (ESS) module, which allows employees to be responsible for the maintenance of their own data and to get access to their information, on their own time, without requiring training on SAP or having core SAP applications on their desktops. SAP Employee Self-Service is fully integrated with SAP Human Resources (HR).

E-Commerce

You should know that electronic commerce represents a huge opportunity for companies. There is the potential for reaching new markets, reducing costs, improving turnaround times, and enhancing relationships with customers and suppliers. Using the Internet, businesses can easily communicate with each other and with their consumers in what is estimated to be a $30 trillion global marketplace by the end of the year 2001 (Peter Bishop, director of international trade at the London Chamber of Commerce, Britain Independent Television Network, Business Section, November 24, 1998; **www.itn.co.uk**). In response to this, SAP has begun to release its own Internet application components.

SAP's Online Store

SAP's online store is a business-to-consumer and business-to-business Internet application component, which enables businesses to offer products online or make purchases themselves. There is a large amount of information about this module on the SAP Web site, and consultants who are in the sales and procurement side of a business are encouraged to learn as much as possible about it.

SAP's Business-to-Business Procurement Module

SAP's Business-to-Business Procurement module is a part of the SAP Supply Chain Management initiative called SCOPE. It is important to remember that this module does not cover just the procurement of materials, but service, maintenance, and repair operations as well.

Wrapping Up

With the explosion of new technologies such as the Internet, intranets, and ERP solutions over the past decade, there is a real shortage of qualified IT personnel. The millennium crisis and the introduction of the Euro have amplified this shortage.

SAP is taking steps to penetrate new markets and change its product to be in step with its customers. Employees and consultants that embrace these changes, practice good consulting techniques (like those mentioned in the following pages), and keep informed should have no problem with steady and profitable employment for many years to come.

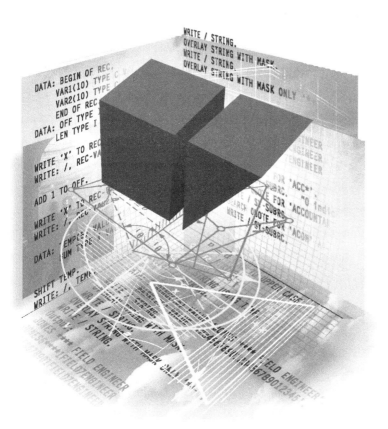

Chapter 2

Résumés

The résumé (sometimes referred to as a *CV* or *curriculum vitae*) is extremely important for an SAP professional because it is your main marketing tool. There are as many different styles of résumés as there are professionals. This chapter discusses two résumé formats that work very well for consulting. Also discussed are things to consider when handing out résumés, how to easily keep your résumé up-to-date, and the standard accepted format for cover letters.

Résumé Format

The format of a résumé must be carefully considered. The agent or client reading your résumé may not understand SAP or the terms used in the industry. They are usually given the task to "find someone to write interfaces to the MM/PP module." Given this task, they go through a set of résumés and try to find the same key words (i.e., "MM/PP" or "interfaces" in the example above). Because of this key word search, it is important to list all of your experience on the résumé. Clients and agents also focus on the companies for whom you have been a consultant. They look for experience with a project similar to the project that they are trying to staff, on the assumption that your learning curve will be shorter as a result of that experience. Another good reason to put key words into résumés is that many agencies now scan résumés and place your information in a database.

Some people say that résumés should never be more than one or two pages long. This doesn't apply to consultants or in countries where a CV is expected to be at least five pages. Consultants can easily work at a half dozen or more different contracts over a few years. This experience will be recent and pertinent and, therefore, must be on the résumé.

We use this general format for our résumés:

- ◆ Vital Information
- ◆ Formal Education
- ◆ Technical Skill Set

- ◆ Brief General Summary
- ◆ Short Contract Summaries

What people want to know about an SAP professional is whether you can get the job done and how much you charge. Agents, human resource departments, and prospective clients skim through many résumés to find candidates with the qualifications that they are looking for. With this format, the reader is given your key information within the top half of the page:

- ◆ **Who you are and how to get in contact with you**
- ◆ **Your qualifications**
- ◆ **Your skills**

With this knowledge, the reader can then decide whether you meet their needs. If you do interest the reader, they can proceed to a short paragraph about you that is followed by a listing of your past successes, all of which enforce what you have said in the first half-page.

A résumé should be honest and consistent. If you list programming languages or modules in your résumé and claim a good deal of experience in them, back up this claim with detail in the work summary section. Listing items on a résumé that are not accurate can lead to disastrous results, as people are sometimes hired based on their résumé alone. The information that should be contained in each section is detailed in the following sections.

Vital Information

Your vital information includes your name, address, phone numbers (home, daytime, and fax), and e-mail address. If you are being marketed via an agency, the agency will likely code your résumé to ensure privacy when a potential client reviews it — or you can ask the agency to do so. Coding your résumé hides your personal information from a client until the client is ready to interview you.

Formal Education

List all your post secondary education, including your diplomas and degrees, SAP classes, SAP certifications, and personal development courses (Stephen Covey, Dale Carnegie, etc.).

NOTE

The formal education section can appear at the end of the résumé as well. See the alternative résumé style later in this chapter for an example and explanation.

Technical Skill Set

Include in this section programming languages, operating systems, SAP versions, and popular software packages that you have strong experience with.

TIP

Remember to include version numbers whenever possible. Listing Microsoft Windows as an operating system that you know can mean experience in Windows 3.1 or Windows 98, two fairly different systems.

Brief General Summary

We usually give a general summary of our consulting strengths and how we can help an organization in this section. This section is important because it provides your only chance to elaborate on your strengths, especially in areas of SAP, and it's also your opportunity to tell of your desire to focus on a specific area. Keep this section to just one or two brief paragraphs.

Contract Listing

This section for consultants contains a list of all of your contracts, starting with the most recent. Things to include are:

◆ Client name. This may need to be listed generically, e.g. *a large manufacturing organization.*

◆ Start/end date of contract. Usually in month/year format.

◆ Project name. This is optional.

◆ Paragraph outlining the scope of your work at the contract and describing your contribution, especially if your added value is more than just writing an interface or configuring. It is important to note your role as advisor, consultant, director, or leader in the client environment. Try to keep the paragraph under five or six lines. Remember to include the various modules of SAP that you were directly involved with.

Some clients also look to see whether there are any gaps in your contract history. If you are a good consultant, gaps will be short. Explain any gaps longer than a few months in the résumé. Your most recent experience counts the most, and you should devote more attention and detail to your latest work. The following pages contain a sample résumé.

Position Listings

For permanent employee positions, the important thing to remember is to list your most recent experience first and to try and show an increasing level of knowledge or responsibility in your progression from one position in a company to another. The first résumé shown on the next page is an example of a generic résumé.

The second résumé layout has the same information, but in a slightly different format. This layout places the education section at the end. Also, a more traditional Objective statement replaces the General Summary section of the first format. You may want to use this style résumé if you have considerable SAP experience, but only limited formal education. By putting the education at the end you will sell the reader on your SAP skills first.

Résumé Omissions

Do not include the following in a résumé:

◆ **References**. Prepare a list of references in a separate document and give this out only if you are fairly well advanced in the interview process. Putting references in a résumé is not recommended, because you cannot be sure who will get a copy of it and you don't want just anyone calling your references. Ideally, you should talk to your references just before they are called.

John Doe
123 Somewhere Dr.
Anyplace, USA 12345
Home (555) 555-5555
E-mail: Doe@internet.com

EDUCATION

Bachelor of Science, Electrical Engineering, University of Somewhere, USA

TECHNICAL SKILLS

ABAP (3.1h), JAVA 6.0, C/C++ 6.0, Microsoft Office 97

GENERAL SUMMARY

I have in-depth knowledge of both the functional and technical areas of MM/PP at a location with complex requirements. Of specific interest to me are projects that have configurable materials, Engineering Change Management, and complex MRP situations.

EXPERIENCE

Lead IT consultant: Large Electronics Manufacturer, CA (07/97 to present).

Lead an MM/PP team of four consultants in implementing a 3.1h SAP installation in a build-to-order manufacturing environment. Responsible for all aspects of the project including initial business requirement scooping, design, code development, documentation, and training. Complicated configurable product structures made this task especially challenging.

Lead IT consultant: Large Oil Company, CA (08/96-06/97)

Primarily worked in Material Management and Warehouse Management to provide the client with the correct configurations and business procedures to follow to meet the client's environment needs.

John Doe
123 Somewhere Dr.
Anyplace, USA 12345
Home (555) 555-5555
E-mail: Doe@internet.com

OBJECTIVE

To apply my in-depth knowledge of both the functional and technical areas of MM/PP at a location that has complex requirements. Of specific interest to me are projects that have configurable materials, Engineering Change Management, and complex MRP situations.

EXPERIENCE

Lead IT consultant: Large Electronics Manufacturer, CA (07/97 to present).

Lead a MM/PP team of four consultants in implementing a 3.1h SAP installation in a build-to-order manufacturing environment. Responsible for all aspects of the project including initial business requirement scoping, design, code development, documentation, and training. Complicated configurable product structures made this task especially challenging.

Lead IT consultant: Large Oil Company, CA (08/96-06/97)

Primarily worked in Material Management and Warehouse Management to provide the client with the correct configurations and business procedures to follow to meet the client's environment needs.

EDUCATION

Bachelor of Science, Mechanical Engineering, University of Somewhere, USA

◆ **Addresses of past clients.** Although listing names of past clients is all right, it is important to keep control and not to let prospective clients get in touch with your past clients without your knowledge. You want to make sure that prospective clients only contact people who know they are a reference and are prepared to talk about you.

◆ **Names of past supervisors.** Just like addresses, it is important to keep control of who has access to your past supervisors.

◆ **Compensation received in the past.** By listing your previous compensation, you are setting an expectation, which may be too low or too high. Also, résumés may accidentally be circulated through offices in which compensation is confidential. If compensation expectations are requested, submit them in a separate letter or include them in a formal cover letter.

Common Résumé Mistakes

As a consultant, your résumé is in constant use and must be perfect. The following are things to check for and to avoid on your résumé:

◆ Misspellings, typographical errors, poor grammar

◆ Irrelevant information such as health or sex

◆ Elaborate fonts, pictures, outlandish paper stock, italics

◆ Too much or not enough information; give enough, but not irrelevant information

◆ Poor type and print smears, which makes the résumé hard to read and looks unprofessional

◆ Unprofessional e-mail addresses or Web site references such as bestsapconsultant@email.com

Keeping It Current

Because of their format, updating the résumés listed in the previous sections is very easy. To update them, you simply ensure that the vital information section is still correct, update your education, and add summaries for your last contract.

Every few years you may want to go through the older contract information in your résumé. As your knowledge of SAP increases, you may find better ways to word the contract information. You may also want to shorten their descriptions as the older contracts start to mean less and less.

Sending to Clients and Agencies

During the first phone conversation, an agent usually asks you to send the agency your résumé. Take this step cautiously! When sending your résumé:

◆ Get an assurance from the agent that the agency will not submit your résumé to a client or share it with another company without your verbal approval. Hopefully, in this way you can control the dissemination of your résumé to the outside world. If you are trying to obtain a contract through several agents, it could happen that the same potential client gets multiple copies of your résumé. This is extremely embarrassing to both you and the agents. If you find out that an agent is circulating your résumé without your permission, contact the agent and let them know that you will not entertain any offers for any position unless you have authorized the résumé for this position.

◆ Find out how your résumé will be presented to a client. Some agencies will either remove your name or put your résumé into their format. If they rework your résumé into their format, get the right to review it before it is sent out to ensure that it is still factually correct and that they did not miss anything.

◆ Avoid using too much formatting. Make your résumé's format as simple as possible. You may have to send your résumé in electronic format to an agent who does not have the same word processor or fonts as you do, or whose e-mail system does not allow attachments, which will require that the résumé be sent in simple, unformatted text. This is especially true for international work.

Sending Résumés for Foreign Assignments

Countries outside of North America usually want additional information on your résumé, such as:

◆ Your marital status, citizenship, country of birth, passport data

◆ Languages that you are fluent in

◆ A handwritten cover letter, which they will use to judge neatness and which they may submit for handwriting analysis

◆ A chronological list of previous contracts starting from your first job and ending with your most recent job, which is exactly opposite to the North American version of your résumé

Cover Letters

While the résumé is a somewhat generic advertisement for yourself that you may send unaltered to many different companies, the cover letter allows you to tailor your application to each specific job. In the current SAP environment, cover letters are not much used. Typically, you contact or are contacted by an agent and your résumé is all that passes hands. However, if you are new to the consulting field or if you find yourself needing to put a cover letter together, a format similar to the one below works well.

In general, the cover letter should be four paragraphs in length and printed on the same quality and color of paper as your résumé. The following is a sample generic cover letter.

Things to Avoid in Cover Letters

Many of the same mistakes that can be made in a résumé also can be made in the cover letter. Make sure that all of the information is accurate, that there are no typographical errors, and do not make the letter look too flashy. The following are mistakes to avoid:

◆ Clichés, amusing anecdotes, and anything else that is not relevant to the position for which you are applying.

◆ Desperation. Instead, make your letter reflect a determined person.

◆ Mentioning your weaknesses. Instead, your cover letter should emphasize your strengths.

◆ Not personally signing your cover letters.

◆ Not ensuring that all information about the prospective employer is correct. Because the cover letter should be specific for the job/employer, make sure that all details in the letter about the employer are accurate.

Your present address
City, state, Zip code
Today's date

Name of person to whom you are writing
His/her title
Company/organization
Street address
City, state, Zip code

Dear Mr. Smith:

1st paragraph: Tell why you are writing; name the position, field, or the type of work for which you are applying. Tell how you heard of the opening or organization and why you decided to contact this employer.

2nd paragraph: Mention your qualifications that you think are of greatest interest to the employer. Tell why you are particularly interested in the company, location, and/or type of work; in other words, tell what you can do for the employer. If you have had related experience, or specialized training, be sure to point it out.

3rd paragraph: Refer the reader to your résumé.

4th paragraph: Close your letter with an indication of what specific action that you desire be done next—usually an interview. Clearly indicate if you expect the employer to take the next step, or if you will take it, and identify what the next step is.

Sincerely,

(your signature)

Type your name

Enclosure: Résumé

Wrapping Up

Your résumé is your most powerful marketing tool. This chapter covers two formats that are easy to update and that work well for contract work. Also discussed are what items to avoid in a résumé and how to handle your résumé as it leaves your hands and goes to an agency for presentation to a client. The cover letter is used in conjuction with your résumé to tailor your experience directly to the client's needs.

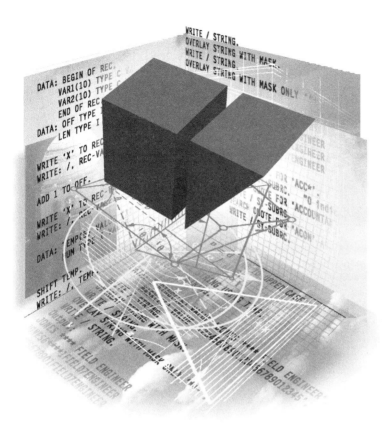

Chapter 3

Interviews

There are several types of interviews that an SAP consultant can participate in, such as interviews with clients, interviews with agents, and interviews with clients as part of a consulting firm. You might also interview for a permanent SAP position. The purpose of this chapter is to outline all of the stages of the interview process and to show how to best prepare for them.

Before the Interview

Before interviewing with a client, find out as much as possible about the client's project and company. Information can usually be obtained from fellow consultants or your marketing representative. Other good information sources are the company's 10Q quarterly fiscal report and the Internet. Even if you cannot get information about the specific company, you may be able to get information about a similar company. The major points you should consider about the company and its SAP implementation include the following:

◆ **Type of business.** What does the company do? Who are its competitors? This can easily be obtained through the Internet, especially on Web sites containing stock information.

◆ **Fiscal status.** Is the company in good shape? Is the stock price increasing or decreasing? If possible, find specific information about the division that you will be interviewing with and compare it to the rest of the company.

◆ **Latest message from the CEO.** Usually you can find some kind of recent statement from the CEO on a company's Web site. This statement can be used to determine the company's short- and long-term goals.

◆ **Version of SAP that the project is targeted for.** Is the company working with a current version of SAP, an older version, or is it planning on implementing a future version?

◆ **Upgrade or new installation.** To some degree, this determines the level of experience the company and its employees currently have with SAP.

- ◆ **Modules to be installed**. This can indicate if this is a full SAP implementation or just a subset. It can also determine the type and complexity of work you will be performing.

- ◆ **Type of hardware and database**. This information can be very important if, for example, you are a Basis consultant with only Oracle experience and the company runs on Informix.

- ◆ **Who will be running the project**. Will the work be done by direct employees of the company or by freelancers?

- ◆ **Estimated length of contract and project**. If these two are different, you can inquire about the possibility of contract extensions. See Chapter 4, "Agents," for more information on contracts and interview preparation.

When you prepare to speak to the client, make sure you ask questions that show that you are familiar with the above points and with SAP projects, such as:

- ◆ What type of manufacturing processing do you currently use: build-to-stock or build-to-order?

- ◆ Are you currently using Engineering Change Control to manage master data changes?

- ◆ Which modules do you have (or are you planning on installing) in your SAP environment?

Prior to the interview, think about the questions that you may be asked and decide how to respond to them. Be prepared for open-ended questions such as:

- ◆ What are your strengths and weaknesses?

- ◆ Why do you want to work here?

- ◆ Where do you see yourself in five years?

- ◆ Why should we hire you?

- ◆ What contributions did you make to your last contract job?

There are also some things that you should do automatically prior to any interview, such as:

- ◆ Review your résumé and make any necessary corrections.

- ◆ Print a few copies of your résumé and bring them to the interview.

- ◆ Print out your references. If you have not spoken to them in a while, give them a call! Bring the reference lists to the interview.

◆ Confirm times, travel arrangements, directions, and phone numbers a few days prior to the interview.

◆ If the interview is a telephone interview, confirm the time, time zone, and who will be calling whom.

Your goal is to be offered a contract or at least to progress to the next interview. When you prepare in advance, you can ask and answer intelligent questions, which impresses interviewers and gives you information to help you decide whether you want this particular position.

Agent Setup Interviews

Frequently, an agent that you have not worked through before sets up your interview with a client. This can lead to problems because the agent probably has not established a contract with the client that specifically outlines your compensation. Usually this is done after the client agrees to bring you on. In this case, you need to tell the agent what your specific compensation requirements are before the interview. Also, you should be prepared to sign an agreement with the agent that you will not hire on with this specific client for the next six months unless it is through the agent. Although this type of agreement is a standard practice in the industry, be careful that there are no other unacceptable clauses in it.

The Interview

The interview itself should be fairly straightforward and, if you have done your homework on the company and the position, should go very smoothly. The consultant's two primary goals during an interview are to:

◆ Obtain adequate information about the job and the organization in order to determine if the job is suitable and desirable.

◆ Impress the employer enough to progress to the next step of the interview process by relaying important information regarding your technical skills and your communications skills.

At the beginning of most interviews are the introductions and a brief rapport-building period. During this phase, you should remember the interviewer(s) name, act relaxed, and participate in the small talk.

Shortly thereafter, the interviewer usually gives general information about the company and the job. At this point, you should absorb as much information as you can about the company and the job. The interviewer also asks general questions about you and your qualifications.

You'll then go into detail about the position and how your skills fit the job. If you have researched the company and paid close attention during the second stage of the interview, you will do well here. At this stage, your goal is to impress the interviewer with your analysis of how your skills set matches the client's exact needs. You also want to discover the job details so that you can determine if this job matches your criteria.

TIP

The main purpose of the interview is to get an offer. You may want to hold back on some of the more specific questions, such as those regarding working hours, so that both you and the client can concentrate first on your compatibility within the company.

The final stage of the interview is the closing. Save a question until the end of the interview. Asking a question at the end of the interview ends it on a positive note and leaves the interviewer with a good impression of you. Conclude the interview by reiterating your interest in the position and how your skills integrate well with the client's needs. Obtain a business card from each person who interviewed you and find out what the next step will be.

Some general tips for all interviews are:

◆ When possible, answer a question in terms of the client's business.

◆ Speak clearly and not too quickly.

◆ Be punctual.

◆ For telephone interviews, make sure that you are in a quiet place and that you will not be distracted or interrupted.

◆ For personal interviews, ensure that you are neat in appearance.

◆ Be positive and show your enthusiasm for the company and your eagerness to apply your skills to get the job done.

Even if you arranged the interview independently or through your own company, do not discuss compensation during the interview. Your interviewer is unlikely to be the right person with whom to discuss this. Also, many companies treat compensation for employees and contractors as confidential information, and management does not want company employees to know how much a consultant is paid. Contract and compensation negotiations are covered in "Negotiating" in Chapter 5, "Contracts."

Interviewing with Agents

Interviews with agents are very straightforward when compared to interviews with clients. When you interview with an agency, you already know that they want to hire you; the only questions are whether they can find the appropriate client for your skills set and whether you can agree on an acceptable compensation package.

Address these points during the interview:

- Clearly outline what traveling you are willing to do
- Find out how many consultants the agency has currently working for it; ask for a name or two, and get in touch with them to get their opinion of the agency
- Find out how many clients the agency has
- Find out how paychecks are issued and expenses are reimbursed
- Find out if they offer training

Once you have convinced the agency that you have qualifications that it can market, the next topic is compensation. You need to ensure that the compensation range that the agency offers is acceptable.

Avoid being the first to come up with a dollar figure. If asked what compensation you are expecting, respond that it depends on the client, the type of work involved, and how much traveling is involved. Or respond that you expect to be paid competitively and then ask what similar consultants are making with the agency. With a little effort, you can probably get the agent to give you at least a compensation range.

TIP

Compensation isn't everything. A contract at a lower rate where you learn new skills may be worth more in the long run.

Regardless of whether you come to an agreement on an exact compensation figure, you should ask for a copy of a typical contract from the agency before you interview with clients. Having an advance copy of the agency contract provides an opportunity to review it for any unacceptable clauses.

After the Interview

After an interview it is important to go through a debriefing. Analyze how the interview went and write out key items such as the people involved and their responsibilities and titles. Make notes on any pertinent information about the company or the SAP project. File this information away for future reference, even if you do not accept this position; SAP projects can last for years and you may want to interview at the same company a year later.

Review how the interview went: Did you stumble over any questions or make any mistakes? Think about how you could have better handled any problem areas. Some things that must be done after each client interview are:

◆ Write personalized thank-you notes to each person who interviewed you; make the letters brief, but outline why you are interested in the position and why you are a good candidate.

◆ If your interview was set up through an agency, contact the agency and go over how the interview went. The agent is in a position to call the client and find out if you are going to get an offer, or if the client has any further questions.

Comparing Offers

Rarely are two contract offers easy to compare, and every consultant has different goals. When comparing offers, only compare what is in front of you in writing.

Do not try to compare an offer in hand to one that an agent is working on but has not sent to you. The following points should be considered when comparing multiple offers.

Money

Consider all monetary aspects of each offer and translate the offers into "after-tax present-value" dollars. This equalizes the compensation differences caused by retirement plans, state taxes, completion bonuses, medical plans, and so forth.

To compute the present value of monetary items that will be paid in the future, such as completion bonuses, use this formula:

$$PV = FV/(1+g)^T$$

Notation:

PV = Present Value (value at beginning of the period)

FV = Future Value (value at the end of the period)

g = Average growth rate per period

T = Number of time periods

For example, if you are offered either an up-front signing bonus of $4,000 or a completion bonus of $5,000 after 2 years, you need to determine what the $5,000 is worth in today's dollars to compare it to the $4,000 bonus value:

$$PV = 5000 / (1 + 0.06)^2$$

You find that the $5,000 bonus has a present value (PV) of $4,450 (assuming a 6% rate of return).

Experience

With the fast pace of change in the information technology environment, it is very important to be current with the latest technologies and to broaden your experience. Taking a short contract at a reduced rate while broadening your experience can translate into future contracts at a much higher rate.

Length of Contract

The importance of the length of a contract cannot be judged easily. Many companies will only give you a three- to six-month contract at first. After that period, if you have proven yourself, there is a chance for contract extensions. The reverse can happen as well. You may be offered a one-year contract but the project is cancelled after six months. All contracts have "release" clauses for both sides.

Travel

Comparing the travel requirements and their effect on your lifestyle is difficult but necessary. If you are married, have kids, or are in a relationship, you may prefer to stay local rather than travel across several time zones every week. Ask yourself how much your sanity, as well as other things (relationship, health, etc.) are worth to you. Although consulting is a tough business, it is possible to balance these issues.

Offer Deadlines

Sometimes one company offers you a position while you are still waiting for a response from another. This offer will have a date (and sometimes even a time) by which you must respond. When faced with this situation, you must either get the offering company to extend the deadline or encourage the other company to present an offer before this deadline occurs.

An offer is usually made first by a phone call. At this stage the contract is generally not yet prepared. During this phone call, work as hard as you can to buy the time to make your decision. You will be excited about getting the offer, but it is important that you be calm and negotiate as long a decision period as possible. Even if you are not expecting another offer, getting this extra time is crucial since it will give you time to analyze your options. After the phone call, the contract is prepared and sent to you.

After you have received a contract, it is more difficult to extend your decision-making period. If you are waiting for another offer, you need to inform that party that you have received an offer that you are seriously considering and that you must respond by a certain date. Ask if there is anything that you can do to speed their decision-making process, such as helping with compensation issues, getting referrals or other documentation (work visas, etc.), or resolving a problem between your agency and them.

If you decide to decline an offer simply because you are waiting for another offer, decline gracefully and make sure that the client knows that you have not turned down the offer because of its terms, but because you are waiting for another client to make an offer. If you subsequently decide that you should accept the declined offer, there is a chance that the client might offer the position to you again.

Wrapping Up

A consultant's interview goals are to get a job offer and enough information about the position to decide whether to accept an offer. A consultant should learn as much about the company and the position as possible before the interview. During the interview, be positive; impress the client and make them believe that they need you because you are a perfect fit for the position.

During client interviews, do not discuss compensation unless necessary. Finally, after the interview, write notes for future reference. When the job offers come in, always try to get as much time as possible to make a decision.

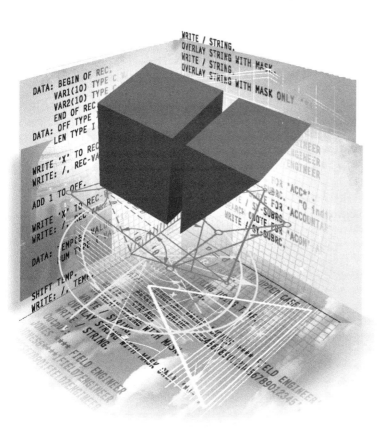

Chapter 4

Agents

Because the SAP market currently has a shortage of qualified individuals, employment agencies have become commonplace in the SAP arena. These agencies represent a variety of clients, ranging from large and small consulting firms to private companies who are hiring independent or full-time employees.

Large Consulting Firms

The *Big Six* firms have consolidated into the *Big Five*, but they are still referred to as the *Big Six*. These five consulting firms are PriceWaterhouseCoopers (PWC), Ernst and Young LLP, KPMG Consulting LLP, Deloitte and Touche LLP, and Arthur Andersen. When a company decides to implement SAP, it usually chooses to have SAP's consulting arm or one of its major partners (all Big Six consulting firms are major partners) guide it through the implementation. Sometimes, however, a company chooses to do the entire implementation on its own.

Most implementations are lead by one of the Big Six. Besides implementing the software, the Big Six firm also devises a budget for the project, a timeline in which the project will be completed, and an analysis which the company will follow to reengineer its business processes. Then, once the planning stages of the project are complete, the firm brings in functional and technical consultants to implement the plan and the SAP software.

Internal Recruiters

There are recruiters who work internally among these big firms. They recruit exclusively for the firm, and are the equivalent of a human resources representative from a private firm.

The question for an SAP consultant is, "How does this individual help my career path in SAP?" For this discussion, we assume that you have chosen to follow a career path that involves working for a large consulting firm.

The internal recruiter has a very good grasp of the openings available inside the consulting firm with which they are associated. The internal recruiter is loyal to the firm he or she works for, and it serves the recruiter's interest to recruit you into that firm. The salary and bonus structure they negotiate for you and many others like you determines their worth to the company. So, when dealing with this individual, you must always consider their motivation to bring you into their company, as they generally recruit you in a manner that will be economically beneficial to the firm.

Our experience is that when dealing with recruiters for large consulting firms, it is good to deal with one of these individuals, although not exclusively. To obtain a position with a large firm, it is in your best interest to create as much leverage as possible with the firms that are interested in you. Dealing with multiple recruiters (at least three) creates a tension amongst them to pay you competitively and induces them to offer other benefits such as training and a higher position within the consulting firm. Not only will these internal recruiters play all their cards, they will go the extra mile to get more for you so that they can recruit you into their firm. A good idea is to include an external recruiter in the mix of people shopping you around, as an external recruiter will offer a whole new perspective on what you are worth, and what to look for in your new position.

External Recruiters

Aside from internal recruiters, employment agencies and agents working for external third-party firms also recruit for large consulting firms. The company that hires you compensates these firms. A firm might tell you that you have to pay them for their services. Decline this offer kindly and remind them that there are hundreds of other such agents with many contacts who do not charge for this service, as the company the agents are recruiting for will pay them.

These companies might have budgeted for the recruiter's fees, but they might try to make this compensation dependent on how good a deal the recruiter gets for them when hiring you. On the other hand, remember that you are a rare talent. The benefit of a third-party recruiter is that they can shop you around to many companies, including large consulting firms, small consulting firms, and private companies. The third-party recruiter provides a single point of contact in dealing with multiple companies. Also, this external recruiter can bid companies against each other without your intervention. However, make sure you know how much you wish to be compensated as well as the career experience you wish to obtain from a new job. Once these issues have been negotiated between you and the agent, discuss these points with your new company to make sure that the external recruiter represented these facts to you accurately. Although many of these recruiters are very charming and amiable, remember that this is a business relationship, not a friendship. The only person who is truly looking out for you is yourself.

There are many external recruiters, and each specializes in recruiting for different types of consulting positions. For example, some deal primarily in recruiting for permanent positions for private firms, others recruit primarily for consulting firms, and others recruit private contractors for consulting and private firms.

Big Six Firm Benefits

A major benefit of working for a large consulting firm is that your job security as an SAP consultant is much higher than that of a private contractor. Your job security as an informational services consultant is preserved because it's to the benefit of the large consulting firm to keep your skill set current and sharp. The consulting firm makes profits from your services, so it is to its advantage to keep you very marketable and valuable to its clients.

If your goal is to work your way up the management ladder in corporate informational services, then large consulting firm experience is very valuable. Most large corporations look at this time spent working with large consultancies as a right of passage into the executive ranks.

When working for a large consulting group, it is likely that you will be working for multiple clients at the same time, whereas an independent consultant usually works for one client at a time. While this might take some adjustment, the contacts that you will make at these companies and in dealing with other consultants are invaluable. Just make sure that you practice your networking skills (See Chapter 11, "Workplace Etiquette") and the large consulting experience will fill your coffers with contacts for your future career.

Big Six Firm Drawbacks

There are also certain tradeoffs in choosing a career within a large consulting firm. As a permanent employee, you generally have the opportunity to remain in one central location while maintaining a job in a specific area for an extended period of time. If being close to family and friends is important to you, then consulting might not be the way to go. As a consultant, your expertise will be needed all over the country, and perhaps throughout the world. Although you will maintain a position in a home office, this office will send you wherever its clients need you. Your employer will consider how far and frequent these trips are, depending on your preferences.

The amount of money you make increases and your job security decreases as you move from permanent employee to consultant to private contractor. Consulting companies make money from lending out your services, charging high hourly rates, and paying you a small percentage of that rate. In exchange, they keep you working and train you. However, you are paid a salary plus bonuses, depending on how well the project does. Overtime is not generally compensated with an hourly rate, but your consulting group keeps the majority of the hourly rate that the company is charged. When you work for a large consulting group, depending on your seniority and experience, you generally make 25 to 50 percent of what an independent consultant makes.

Representing Your Firm

How is working as an independent consultant different than working as part of a large consulting team? The difference lies in the fact that you are not representing only yourself in this endeavor, but a team of consultants and the entire culture of the consulting firm. You must play the role of consultant, but in terms of the values by which your consulting company wishes to be represented. In many cases, this takes more effort and time than your functional purpose on the SAP implementation.

Small to Midsize Consulting Firms

There is another choice between going independent and working for a large consulting group. Small to midsize consultancies, started by executives from SAP or former high-level managers or partners of large consulting groups, are becoming more and more prominent as players in the SAP industry.

If you want to work in a small-company environment where you won't get lost in the crowd, then a small consulting group may be for you. The positives that may come with this type of atmosphere include more recognition for your efforts and potentially more money than working for a large consulting group.

On the negative side, some recruiters lease out talent (you) to their clients, but then want to pay that talent (you) on a salary basis. This setup gives you all the disadvantages of being an independent consultant (salary, no training, little benefits) and none of the advantages of being in a real consulting group (training, benefits, prestige). These types of small consultancies are generally referred to as *body shops*. Working for such groups gives you no or very little training and no team to work with. For this "privilege" you would generally receive a smaller salary with the same job security as an independent consultant. (The general rule is that if budget cuts hit a company, the consultants are cut first, with the independent consultants being the first of the first. The consulting firms work hard in such circumstances to keep their consultants as long as possible at the client's site.)

Agent/Consultant Relationships

When an agent first comes to you with a job proposal, there are certain things you should ask before you decide to move forward and do an interview with the client or negotiate the contract.

- ◆ **Where is the project?** If you wish to stay local, then this is an important question to ask. You can always ask your agent to keep the sites local that they refer you to.

- ◆ **What is the project's job description?** Rather than going to an interview to find that the job is different than what you are qualified for, try to find that out up front.

- ◆ **What version of SAP are they implementing?** If you are an SAP version 4.5 expert, and the client is still implementing 3.0, then you might want to think twice about doing the project, as your skills will become stagnant. Or, in exchange for that stagnation, you can request a larger sum of money.

- ◆ **What modules is this company implementing?** This will help you decide whether you are qualified for the position, or if you can prepare yourself for it. If you are somewhat familiar with the modules, then you may want to accept the position and increase your skill set.

- ◆ **Where are they in their current R/3 implementation, and how long has it lasted so far?** The agent might offer a contract that lasts for six months to a year, but if the project is almost completed, you might want to consider how long it will actually last. Also, with this knowledge, you can ask the client how long your services will actually be needed.

◆ **How long is the contract for?** Clients will offer three-month, six-month, and sometimes year long contracts. While the project might last six years, your services will initially be needed only for the term of the contract. The rule of thumb is not to sign for a contract of less than six months if you desire some stability.

◆ **What is the rate?** The agent will dance around this question, asking you what you would like to make. Have a number in mind (either a daily or hourly rate), and keep in mind that the agent will charge a percentage on top of your billable rate. Ask them what percentage they generally take home. Sometimes agents go through several other agents to fill positions, which may involve two to four people taking cuts of your pay.

◆ **Is the company willing to pay for travel expenses?** If travel is involved, then make sure this is covered. This is standard in the industry, so do not fall for a company saying that it will pay you X number of dollars per hour/day, and part of that is to cover your expenses. We always state that we want X number of dollars, plus expenses on top of that. The company is free to pay us Y number of dollars extra, or reimburse us for plane fare, food, and lodging.

◆ **Is this job a W-2, 1099, or corporation job?** See Chapter 8, "Financial Planning," for more information. If you are charging the agent or client through a corporation, then you want to ask for more money to cover your self-employment tax as well as social security.

Agent Trust

As you develop a relationship with an agent, you will slowly develop the trust of that agent. Agents are generally very people-oriented and very charming, but remember that they are in this business to make money for themselves. By asking the questions listed in the previous section, you will have the facts you need. If an agent misrepresents any major facts, halt your business with them without burning your bridges. A simple, "thank you, but I have another agent I am going with" is enough of an explanation.

Consultation before Representation

Make sure that the agents representing you do not send your résumé to the same companies. Duplicate representation often disqualifies you from employment consideration by those companies. To prevent this, have the agents ask your permission before submitting your résumé to a company. Be sure to keep track of which agents have submitted your résumé to which companies. If two agents submit your résumé to the same company, that company is unlikely to consider you for employment because it does not wish to be a part of the squabble between the two agents.

Enter the consulting world with a positive, cautious attitude. When you deal with a current or new agent, assume that they will represent and take care of you in a proper manner. If they disappoint you, then they risk losing your business. If they go the extra mile for you, you'll keep this in mind in your future dealings with them, and reward them for their work.

A Guide to Tracking Quality

One of our college professors made the point that in investing he would find a mutual fund with a great performance, and then invest in the funds that that mutual fund manager manages. He was not loyal to the specific company that held that mutual fund, but rather to the individual who made that mutual fund what it is. If the mutual fund manager moved companies, our professor would move his money to the new mutual funds being managed by that individual.

One thing worth noting is that if you are on a job that you have been placed in by a particular agent, depending on their client relationship, they may not be able to recruit you out of that particular client. The danger here is assuming that a recruiter is working hard for you when in reality they aren't doing much because they don't want to jeopardize their client relationship. Of course, there are exceptions, but the same rule applies to consulting and agents. If you find a good agent to represent you, stick with them. If they leave their company, make sure that you get their new contact information. Chances are you'll build a beneficial relationship with that person.

Referrals

Agents generally offer a bonus if you refer a consultant to them who fills an open position. Some agents offer $200 for such a referral, some offer $5,000, and the average is about $1,000.

Companies impose terms on these referrals that have to be met before they pay the referral bonus, usually that the consultant must stay on the job for at least two to three months. It is a good idea to ask the agent for a signed contract saying that in exchange for the referral of consultant ABC, he agrees to pay you X number of dollars payable upon Y number of days of ABC's employment.

Expenses

Expenses are either paid as a per diem (see Appendix B, "Per Diem Rates") or reimbursed to you from your agency or from the client. These expenses range from airfare to telephone calls. Keep track of your receipts (write on the back of them if they are company-related) and submit them each month in an expense report. The client or your agent will reimburse you.

Per Diems

Per diems (dollars per day) are a way for a company to pay for your expenses, travel, food, lodging, and so forth (see Appendix B, "Per Diem Rates"). Check with your local IRS office or on the Web at **www.irs.gov** for a schedule of the maximum dollars per diem for your locale.

The IRS allows a per diem for one year of employment for a certain client in a certain location working as a W-2 employee. If you will be traveling and working for a client for more than one year as a W-2 employee of your agent, then you might want to find a way to be compensated after that year, as the IRS will tax that per diem as income to you. Consult your tax attorney or accountant for more details on per diems and tax-related information.

Travel

Generally, you must negotiate travel arrangements early on in the negotiations, but most clients accept the fact that they must fly their consultants in each week or every second week. The company will either book the tickets for you or reimburse you for any travel arrangements you make, as long as you send in the receipts of the travel with your expense report.

 NOTE

Your client sometimes also pays for meals and telephone calls. Generally, your agency or the client will give you a certain dollar limit for meals. Most clients also let you use their telephone for long distance calls back home, as long as you do not abuse this privilege.

Calling It Quits

If for some reason you wish to quit or terminate your contract, then there are certain things to consider. What does your contract say about early termination, and what penalties would it impose? What would the ramifications be on the relationship between you, your client, and your agent?

While it might be fun before quitting to get on the phone and tell your agent what you really think of them, or perhaps tell the client how they really should run their project, this isn't advisable. Regretfully inform them that you are giving notice that in a certain number of weeks you will be working at another client's implementation. They will remember you for your projects as well as how you act in your last few days. Be pleasant to work with and have a smile on your face until you walk out the door for the final time.

When considering whether you should quit (assuming that your current contract is not ending), try to determine if your current skill set will improve on a new job. Training or exposure to new technology is a good reason to pursue another position, especially if you are stagnating at your current position.

Also consider how much you enjoy working at your present site and with your current team. If you hate going to work every day because of the people you work with and the projects to which you are assigned, this feeling is probably reflected in your work. Look for another contract site at which you will enjoy yourself and work on the projects you enjoy.

There is always the allure of more money around the corner. But not all of that money is profit. The new job might pay you $10 an hour more, which translates to roughly $20,000 more per year. However, it might be three time zones away from your family. Determine what the new job is worth to you and try to maximize its benefits.

Wrapping Up

Agents are a very important tool in your SAP career. You are wanted, and they are the people who will find out where you are truly wanted and what your services are worth to others. Do not be upset that they are making money off of you. As your networking skills grow, perhaps you will be able to place yourself, but be thankful of the service they provide you for the present. Once you develop a good relationship with an agent, they can be very powerful allies in building your exciting new SAP career.

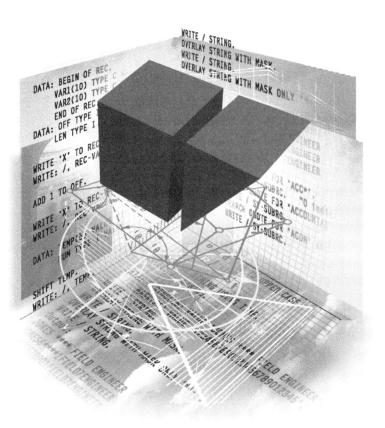

Chapter 5

Contracts

When you agree to work for a company as a consultant, the company will ask you to sign an employment contract. These contracts are designed to protect your rights, the rights of the company you are contracting with, and the rights of the client company for which you will be working.

We discuss in this chapter the necessary ingredients of a contract, as well as the clauses that you must either avoid or at least be wary of. In addition to these clauses, there are clauses that you can use as leverage or bargaining tools when negotiating. As there will also be many legal and technical issues involved, we recommend that you retain a lawyer to review and negotiate your contract as well.

Contractual Necessities

The best contract is plainly worded, easy to understand, and prints out on about one page. It spells out that you will work for the client for X number of months and be paid Y number of dollars on this day of each month.

There are certain contract clauses that you should include in the agreement. The first contractual necessity is that the rate (daily or hourly) at which the contract agency will pay you for your services is stated in the contract.

 NOTE

The billing rate is a separate rate written in a separate contract between the contract agency and the client. Generally, you are not privy to the contract specifics between the client and the agency. If this is a problem for you, then you might want to find a consulting group or agency which does disclose this information. Agents might charge anywhere from 15% to 50% of your rate.

If you are signing up for a daily rate, find out how many hours they expect you to work per day, and make sure the contract reflects this. If you are making $1,200 per day and working a 16-hour day, then your rate might not be what you think it should be. (Generally, a daily rate is for an 8- to 10-hour day.) On the other hand, if that $1,200 is for a 10-hour day, you can reach an agreement with your employer for billing the additional six hours.

Second, make sure that the contract states your pay frequency. Some of our colleagues signed a contract only to discover that they were paid each month rather than every week, so they waited two months before receiving a paycheck for their first month.

Third, make sure the contract states how long the contract will last. While the best contracts state that the contract exists by will of both the contractor and the contracting agency (which means that you can leave at any time and that you can be terminated at any time), it is still a good idea to discuss with the client and contracting agency the contract's duration, and verify this in the contract.

Fourth, make sure the contract has a clause which explicitly states how expenses will be handled (i.e. travel, per diem, etc.). In addition to the expense clause, you will also want the contract to spell out the other financial benefits such as 401k plans and deferred compensation packages.

Finally, make sure a clause is included which specifies the perks you will receive with this company (i.e. training allowance, sick time, vacation time).

Contractual Liabilities

There are several clauses that contracting or consulting agencies include in their contracts that may hinder your career as an SAP consultant. It is in your best interests to have these clauses removed before you sign.

The first clause is the noncompete clause, which states that you agree only to do business with this particular client through this contracting agency. If you do not, then it spells out consequences and damages to be paid to the contracting agency. It generally also spells out a time period for this clause to be in effect. Why give your contracting agency this exclusivity? They may be the best agency in the world, but you never want to give up your freedom to pick clients. Remember that someone who does not represent you in the best manner could tomorrow buy out the contracting agency and you would still be bound by that clause! If you are willing to give up this freedom, and you desperately need this job, then sign. However, you currently have a lot of other options to work elsewhere.

The second questionable clause involves your early termination of the contract to join as a permanent employee the company you are contracted to, for which you could be fined. If you choose to become a permanent employee, then the client should arrange for a fee to be paid to the contracting agency. You should arrange this clause so that you don't have to pay any money yourself. The clause should not be present on your contract, but rather between the client and agent. It is in your best interest that your new company pay if you hire on with them.

A third clause to remove is one that penalizes you for leaving a contract before it expires. As a rule of thumb, you should finish your contract and not leave the client hanging. But there are times when you might want to manage an early exit, and you should not be penalized by your contracting agency for doing so. Some contracts require that to avoid a penalty, a minimum amount of notice be given before you leave the client. While giving notice may be the lesser of two evils, it is not something that should be in your contract.

Some clauses state that a certain percentage of the rate will be retained in an interest-bearing account for the duration of the contract, and upon completion, a bonus of that amount will be paid to the consultant. This method is a more friendly approach to encouraging you to stay the entire duration of the contract.

Another clause that you should remove is an exclusivity agreement with a contracting agency, which states that you promise to only seek contracts through that particular contracting agency. In essence, you give up all your freedom to that agency, and you aren't allowed to leverage contracting agencies against each other or go to a client that is not represented by your particular agency.

One standard contractual clause that the client will most likely have you agree to on a separate form is a nondisclosure clause. This clause essentially states that you will not release any client secrets (personnel names, programs, practices, etc.) to anyone outside of the client.

TIP

Review your contract to find out which state's laws govern the contract and then ask an attorney familiar with the laws in that state how you are affected by those laws.

Some agencies have a clause at the end of the contract that states that you agree to be bound by the agency's home state's laws. Just as you are bound to the tax laws of the state you are working in, you are bound to the same state laws as well, so you should delete this statement from the contract.

The Exception to the Rule

If you are working in Pennsylvania, which is not a right-to-work state, and your agency is in Texas, then to be bound by Texas law would not be a bad thing. This is definitely the exception rather than the rule. If the agency wants you bound by a state law that is to your benefit, go for it!

Finally, make sure there is a job-specific exception clause written into your contract which allows you to pursue outside interests (such as book writing!) without breaking your contract.

Negotiating

Negotiating is a skill you will have to develop as your skillset as an SAP professional grows. The big question now that you have a proposed contract sitting in front of you is "What do I agree to despite my wishes and what do I want to negotiate for?" Simply put, you want to negotiate to minimize restrictions and make sure you are compensated adequately.

The contract negotiation process should not be an arduous task. You should make sure that you are reimbursed for any expenses that you will incur (such as travel and food) and that you are paid at the rate that you have negotiated. You should make sure that you are not bound by any of the restrictive clauses previously mentioned. Remember that you are a desired commodity and there are many other agencies out there who would love for you to work with them and would not restrict you with these clauses.

To get what you need, stick to your guns. Say to your agency, "I have reviewed the contract and have found the following clauses to be unacceptable. They need to be removed or rephrased as I have written them." If they say that the client is getting anxious, remind them that you are a willing participant and that they are stalling the process. Remind them that if the contract does not go through, they will lose X percent of the take of the hours you will bill. If you are firm in your wording, you will slowly wear down the agency and it will change its tune. During the negotiations, the agency's representative will be trying to read you, trying to figure out whether or not you will budge. If they get the sense that you are not serious, they will wear you down. As in all negotiations, be willing to walk from the table and say that you can do better elsewhere (if you have something else in the works).

As an SAP consultant, you don't need to accept conditions with which you are uncomfortable. Currently, and for the next several years, your skills are and will be highly sought after, so unless your agent is willing to remove the clauses that are binding, it's time to find another agent.

FAQs

There are certain questions that you should ask your agent or your client:

What will my rate be? Ask this only of the agency, not the client. (Generally, clients do not know how much you make, only how much the agency will charge them.) Before you speak to the client, be sure to specify and negotiate the rate you need from the agent. Otherwise once the client meets you and decides they need you, if the negotiation process starts then, the agent might decide to try to negotiate you down and push the client up, creating a wider spread and larger profit for the agent.

When will the client need my services? You need to know when you have to give notice at your present contract if you are currently under contract (see Chapter 10).

TIP

Keep all your notes about the negotiations handy so that if a dispute arises, you can rely on the facts that you wrote down at the time of the negotiations rather than your memory.

Be sure to read your contract after all the changes that you have negotiated for have been added, removed, and changed. Despite all your conversations, you are responsible for the contract that you are about to sign and be bound by in your next employment venture. The person making changes to your contract is human, and can make mistakes. This is a time to be *very* detail-oriented, because a mistake at this point could cost you a great deal down the road.

Wrapping Up

Doing your job is often only 25% of the work. If you start a job and the clauses you have signed are awful, then the job, no matter how much you enjoy it, will become intolerable. You must negotiate the clauses you want and do not want in your contract. Be sure to stand firm on certain issues, and use other clauses you can bargain with as leverage to get what you want.

It is imperative that you read the final draft of your contract, which contains the rules by which you must play. Finally, retain a lawyer who is astute in the area of contract law and have them advise you on the contract's soundness. What might seem to cost a lot right now can cost much more later if you do not negotiate a good contract. Be sure that the current laws where you work do not bind you into anything you do not want to do.

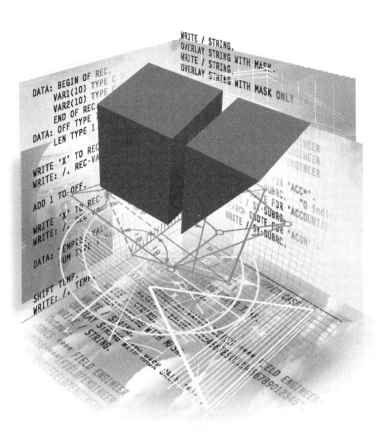

Chapter 6

Working Abroad

Working and travelling abroad can be fun and rewarding. The high demand for SAP consultants makes it relatively easy to find employment in other countries. This is true for both people wanting to work in the United States and for U.S. citizens who wish to work abroad. This chapter discusses finding international work and many of the items to consider when relocating to a different country for a temporary assignment.

What It Takes to Be Successful

Before applying for international jobs, do a self-evaluation to see if you are really cut out for it. To be successful in international work, you need strong internal motivation to adapt to a new environment and to accept the inevitable setbacks that will occur. You also need patience; not everything will go smoothly, especially during the first few months of an overseas assignment.

On many foreign assignments, many of the corporate and social support structures that you are used to will be absent. You must be able to work independently, with self-reliance and initiative. Decisiveness is also a requirement, as you will face many strange and confusing situations.

To succeed in international work, it takes more than a sound knowledge of SAP. It requires having personal traits that allow you to function and thrive in unusual

---

No Credit?

One of the biggest complaints from foreigners working in the United States is they can't get a credit card. Even with a clean credit history in their home countries and a good income in the United States, many are turned down for at least the first six months. Bring a credit report from your home country before you leave and include it (along with letters and supporting documentation) with your credit card application.

Is it worth it?

There are many positives and negatives in international work. In determining if it is right for you, consider the following:

◆ You'll have time to develop rewarding personal relationships with people of a different culture.

◆ Broaden your SAP experience. You will expand your knowledge on how foreign companies operate and how SAP works in different environments.

◆ Save money. Depending on the contract, much of your personal expenses may be paid for.

◆ Lack of social support structure. Even though you may try to keep in touch with friends and relatives back home, they are not as close any more. You will miss holidays, birthdays, anniversaries, etc.

◆ Increased awareness. You must pay extra attention to everything you do since customs, laws, and nearly everything else may not be quite as you are used to.

---

environments. You must also go into this area with your eyes open to both the good and bad aspects of international work.

Finding International Work

One of the first challenges that you face when trying to find international work is that of acquiring a list of contacts that will have employment in the region of the world where you want to work. The type of contacts you want depends on a number of factors, the most important being your level of experience and where you want to work.

One of the easiest ways to find international work is to go with one of the Big Six firms (see "Large Consulting Firms" in Chapter 4).

These firms have both the contacts and resources that make finding a position and relocating quite easy. Many international companies use the Big Six to roll out their worldwide SAP installations because these consulting firms have offices worldwide and are familiar with installations on an international scale. These consulting firms have departments that deal on a daily basis with international tax laws, relocation, obtaining work visas, and so forth, and will do most of this work for you.

Another excellent source for finding international work is the Internet. Some caution should be used, however, as the agency that you are contacting may be unfamiliar to you. See Appendix A, "SAP Internet Resources," for a comprehensive list of Web sites to start you on your job hunt. The first thing that an agency will request from you is a copy of your résumé. Before sending it to the agency, however, make sure you inform the agency not to submit it to any company or other agency without your knowledge. Other do's and don'ts for resumes can be found in Chapter 2, "Resumes."

If you do find a list of jobs that look promising in the country that you are interested in, you may want to arrange for a vacation to this country for in-person interviews. If you are offered a job, you may be able to start work right away, or you may have to return from your vacation for a few weeks until the proper work visa paperwork has been processed (depends on the country).

Most SAP implementations have consultants working on them from other countries. Ask these individuals for information on international job opportunities or for recommendations for reputable agencies. They have first-hand knowledge about a particular job or agency, and this is definitely preferred over answering ads for jobs that you know little about or through agencies with which you have no previous experience.

Consultants from different countries are also a source of advice in the areas of relocation, cost of living, and income taxes in various parts of the world. Even if you are not currently looking at their country for relocation, it is a good idea to find out as much as you can. Specific items to ask about when talking to international consultants include:

◆ **Medical systems.** How do they work? How is the insurance handled? Are there places to avoid?

◆ **Education systems.** Are they similar to where you currently are? Can credits or grade levels be easily transferred to other countries? Are the schools private or public?

◆ **Places to live.** Where are the best areas to live? Are there any legal implications that you should know about for renting or leasing a property?

Another route to consider for finding an overseas placement is applying for a position with SAP itself. In general, working for SAP has the same advantages as working for a Big Six firm.

Table 6-1 lists the countries in which SAP has a standardized version of its software. You will find companies with SAP installed in many other countries as well, but these other installations have add-ons to handle the specific country's specifications that may not be supported directly by SAP.

Table 6-1 Countries with Standardized Versions of SAP

Country	Version	Country	Version
Argentina	4.5A	Mexico	4.5A
Australia	4.5A	Netherlands	4.5A
Austria	4.5A	New Zealand	4.5A
Belgium	4.5A	Norway	4.5A
Brazil	4.5A	Peru	4.5A
Bulgaria	3.0F	Philippines	4.5A
Canada	4.5A	Poland	4.5A
Chile	4.5A	Portugal	4.5A
China	4.5A	Romania	3.1H
Colombia	4.5A	Russia	4.5A
Croatia	3.0D	Saudi Arabia	4.5A
Cyprus	4.5A	Singapore	4.5A
Czech Republic	4.5A	Slovak Republic	4.5A
Denmark	4.5A	Slovenia	3.0F
Finland	4.5A	South Africa	4.5A
France	4.5A	South Korea	4.5A
Germany	4.5A	Spain	4.5A
Greece	3.1H	Sweden	4.5A
Hong Kong	4.5A	Switzerland	4.5A
Hungary	4.5A	Taiwan	4.5A
India	3.1H	Thailand	3.1H
Indonesia	4.5A	Turkey	3.1H
Ireland	4.5A	Ukraine	4.5A
Israel	3.0F	United Arab Emirates	4.5A
Italy	4.5A	United Kingdom	4.5A
Japan	4.5A	United States	4.5A
Luxembourg	4.5A	Venezuela	4.5A
Malaysia	4.5A		

One final way to get into the international arena, especially if your experience level is low, is to get a local position with a company that is rolling out an SAP solution worldwide. When interviewing with them, express your interest in travel. Many consultants do not want to do extensive traveling, and expressing your desire in this area may help you in landing a contract.

There are differences between North America and the rest of the world as to what is expected in a résumé. Before applying for international work, see "Sending Résumés for Foreign Assignments" in Chapter 2.

If you are dealing with an agency (a company not included in the Big Six or SAP itself), investigate the agency to ensure that it is reputable and make sure you understand as much as possible about the contract position. Many international agencies are one- or two-person companies that recruit for larger companies. Such a situation leads to a lower rate percentage, and can lead to complications later if there is a dispute with one of the contracts (either between you and the agency, between the agency and the other consulting firm, or between the consulting firm and the client). Sometimes it is impossible to avoid the small agencies, in which case, you'll need to compensate them. This is usually done through a pass-through rate, where the agency gets a percentage of your hourly rate. If you do go through one of these placement firms, you will want to make sure that the percentage pass-through rate is low (no more than 10%). You should also avoid having multiple levels between you and the actual company that is employing you at the client site. As an alternative, you could also offer the agency a one-time fee for placing you, and not a percentage of your rate. To their advantage, they would have one less set of contracts to worry about. The chances of getting this are low, but it can sometimes be done.

Contracts are important for international work, but remember that if there are problems, the cost of litigating international contracts is high because there are usually two or more countries involved, each with its own set of laws. This, combined with traveling and the translation of languages, increases the cost of litigation to the point where it may not be worthwhile. Therefore, the reputation of the firm that you will be dealing with is very important, even more so than when you deal with an agent in your own country.

Limited Liability Companies

An LLC (Limited Liability Company) is a type of company that is slowly becoming accepted in the US, but is more common in Europe, Asia, and South America.

An LLC is a legitimate front for you to do business in another country and avoid some of the employment hassles of being an employee for someone else.

One-person limited liability companies and offshore companies are not welcome everywhere in Europe, so exercise caution with such companies. An agreement with a limited liability or offshore company sometimes poses problems in obtaining work visas in the destination country. It is easier to work under a company that is set up to pay local taxes and social security.

For these reasons, we suggest that you get professional advice from multiple sources before considering these companies. People that you should talk to include corporate lawyers in the country where you are seeking work and tax attorneys in your current country of residence.

Work Visas

Most countries require some type of work permit to enable you to work there on a temporary basis. It is your responsibility to know about the regulations and requirements regarding work visas. Never take this matter too lightly and always ensure you get qualified legal advice before applying to any government agency regarding visas.

Usually visas are for a set amount of time. Always give plenty of time for visa renewal and apply for the renewal as soon as possible. Delays can also occur for reasons that are beyond your control.

Visas and You

A few years ago, a European friend of ours with a green card was working in the United States, living with his girlfriend, whose student visa had expired. One Christmas, they returned to Europe for a vacation. On returning to the US, the immigration official asked our friend's girlfriend if she intended to move back to Europe soon. She replied that it depended on where her boyfriend found work. Wrong answer! The official, seeing that her boyfriend had a green card, assumed she intended to stay in the United States, and she was denied entry. Even after some legal haggling, she is still barred from re-entry into the United States, even as a visitor.

Working around the Problem

After the 1997 bombings of the American consulates in Africa, many U.S. embassies around the world were closed to visa applications and processing. This left many consultants (and permanent employees) stranded outside the United States because they could not renew their work visas. Some friends of ours who were having trouble extending their visas in Europe simply routed their flights through Canada, where U.S. embassies were open, and had their visas extended there. As a consultant, know that there are always work-arounds, even in life.

The following are are some tips on working visa requirements in various countries. You should always seek the advice of an experienced visa attorney, but it is helpful to know the visa basics when talking to your attorney.

Canada

Citizens of the United States can work up to 180 days in Canada without a work visa. For assignments longer than this, or for people outside the United States, there is a temporary work visa that can take up to one month to process (depending on the applicant's citizenship).

United States

Citizens of Canada can take advantage of NAFTA to work in the United Status through a TN visa. To qualify for a TN visa, you must have a post secondary degree, a valid passport, and a letter of employment from a company in the United States. Family that will be joining you in the U.S. will enter under a TD visa, but will not be able to work in the United States. The initial TN and TD visas are obtained at any valid border crossing into the United States.

At your first entry into the United States, you will be asked to show your letter of employment, a copy of your university degree, a copy of your résumé, and you'll need to pay a small application fee (currently under US $100.00). The TN and TD visas are issued at once. The TN and TD visas are valid for one year and can be renewed for many years, either at a border crossing or through the mail. When renewing through the mail, request a copy of the I-129 form through one of the

INS offices or through its Internet site, and the INS will mail you one. Once you have the forms, you and your employer need to fill them out carefully, send in all requested materials (copy of passport, initial TN entry card, copy of diploma, etc.) along with the processing fee. You can start the mail-in process when there are less than four months remaining on your current visa.

If for some reason your visa expires and your renewal has not been processed, you are not required to leave the United States. However, if you do leave the United States, you will not be able to re-enter until you have a valid visa. One other advantage that Canadians have with a TN visa is that they can work as W-2 hourly contractors or as incorporated entities.

Citizens of countries other than Canada must work in the United States through an H1-B visa (this includes Mexico, even though it is a part of NAFTA). This visa is usually granted for an initial period of three years and can be renewed for another three years. To qualify for an H1-B visa, you need one of the following:

◆ A university degree with computer-related courses and three years of related experience

◆ A college diploma and substantial experience, the sum of which should be equivalent to twelve years of experience in the industry

◆ At least twelve years of experience in the industry.

The processing of the H1-B visa is more complicated than the processing of a TN visa and should be handled by an immigration attorney. Once the six years are up, you must leave the country for one year before returning on a new H1-B. Unfortunately, there are two factors that make it difficult to work in the United States with an H1-B visa. The first is the processing time for getting the visa itself. In the consulting world, clients want new consultants immediately and usually do not want to wait a few months for the H1-B visa processing. The second factor is the tightening of the number of H1-B visa holders that are allowed in the United States each year. Although the cap has been increased for the next few years, there is more demand than capacity, and your application may have to wait until the next batch of H1-B visas are processed. Spouses and other family members are automatically issued an H4 visa, which allows them entry but does not allow them to work in the United States.

There are ways around the complexities and time delays of the H1-B visa. The first is to get an agency to hold the H1-B for you and pay you an hourly rate. This arrangement usually leads to a slightly lower hourly rate, but does allow you to move between contracts since you are still really employed by the agency. Another way to get into contracting work in the U.S. is to take a pay cut for a few years and become a permanent employee. During this time, you can work through the green card process and then switch to contract work.

Australia

Australia's temporary residence program is designed to allow overseas people to come to Australia for specific purposes, which result in some benefit to Australia. The focus is on the areas of skilled employment, and social, cultural, and international relations.

Temporary residents are required to pay taxes on income earned in Australia. They do not have access to social welfare benefits or national public health coverage. Included in the criteria to be met in all of the temporary resident visa classes is that the applicant must be assessed as satisfying Australia's strict good health and character requirements.

The visa that will best suit your needs is the Business (Long Stay) visa, which is valid for between three months and four years. This visa must be sponsored either by a company in Australia wishing to contract your services or by a company outside of Australia that wishes to establish a new business that is of benefit to Australia.

Asia

Work visas in Asia are relatively difficult to get unless you are associated with a large organization. Also, the requirements and laws associated with the work visas vary widely among the countries. If your goal is to work in Asia, your best bet is to work for an organization that is used to dealing in this area.

Europe

The requirements for work visas in Europe vary from country to country. In general, it must be proven that there is a high demand for the position you are applying for, and the process usually takes a few months to complete. Most visas are between a specific company and you, and do not allow for switching to different companies or to a different visa. There are exceptions to this. The United Kingdom has a fast track work-permit program that can be processed in as little as two weeks, valid for up to four years.

Tax Laws

The total amount of taxes to be paid is a very important part of any decision on an international job offer. Not only should you look at the national income tax, but also the state, provincial, or regional tax. Most countries tax based on worldwide income once you establish residency in the country.

U.S. Tax Laws on Foreign Assignments

U.S. citizens or permanent residents are taxed on their worldwide income. There can be a tax incentive for working as a U.S. citizen outside of the United States. In 1999, you may be entitled to exclude up to $74,000 (this amount is indexed and goes up to $80,000 after 2001) of foreign-earned income, in addition to possibly deducting for certain housing costs.

NOTE

For more detailed information, refer to the IRS tax publication 54 and your accountant.

Tax Rates in Other Countries

Tax laws vary widely from country to country. It is very important that you understand the exact tax consequences of working in a country before accepting an assignment. Obtain this information from a qualified international tax attorney. Before contacting an attorney, you may want to get some background information on the tax laws for the country on the Web. A good starting place is usually the government Web site for the specific country. By doing a little bit of legwork yourself, you can then talk more intelligently with your tax attorney.

Each country has its own tax rules which differ among tax rates, income bases, and timing of income recognition. Most countries tax their residents based on their worldwide income and tax nonresidents based on their income that is earned within the country. To avoid double taxation (tax paid twice on the same income), many countries have tax treaties, or at least a foreign tax credit, with other countries. See IRS publication 901 for more detailed information on U.S. tax treaties.

The following is a list of countries that currently have tax treaties with the United States:

Armenia	Greece	Norway
Austria	Hungary	Pakistan
Azerbaijan	Iceland	Philippines
Belarus	India	Poland
Belgium	Indonesia	Portugal
Canada	Ireland	Romania
China	Italy	Spain
Commonwealth of Independent States	Jamaica	Sweden
	Japan	Switzerland
Cyprus	Kazakhstan	Tajikistan
Czech Republic	Korea	Trinidad and Tobago
Denmark	Kyrgyzstan	Tunisia
Egypt (Arab Republic)	Luxembourg	Turkmenistan
England	Moldova	Ukraine
France	Morocco	United Kingdom
Germany	Netherlands	Uzbekistan

Foreign Client Expectations

Many people have a tendency to exaggerate their abilities when writing their résumé. You do not want to do this when applying for a foreign assignment. You want to ensure that you are qualified for the position that you are applying for. The cost of posting an employee overseas adds up quickly with airfare, moving, settling-in allowance, cost of dependents, housing, salary, and so forth. If you are not qualified for the position and this is not determined until after you are accepted and moved, it will be costly for both the client and yourself. This will also leave a bad mark on your current work history, which will make finding the next assignment that much tougher.

International Differences in SAP

Even if you are an expert in a certain portion of SAP in one country, you must be on the lookout for country-specific features in SAP, including:

◆ Chart of accounts

◆ Depreciation methods

◆ Tax calculations

◆ Withholding taxes

◆ Typical local and legal reporting requirements

◆ Material valuation

◆ Sales processing

◆ Human resources payroll

Another area to consider when working on international SAP solutions is the design of bolt-on solutions to the standard SAP system. An SAP consultant should always be aware of the following:

◆ **Multiple languages.** This means no hard coded strings in ABAP programs and always having a language key field in tables that contain text descriptions.

◆ **Multiple currencies.** The most common problem here is in the area of reporting. If you are writing a reporting program that will be used in several countries, ensure that enough room is provided wherever a monetary amount is printed.

◆ **Date format.** In Europe and Canada, the commonly expected date format is Day, Month, Year versus the expected Month, Day, Year format in the United States. Although the user profile does take care of the date display issue, you must be careful when dealing with interfaces that read and write dates to files and to not hard code "MM/DD/YYYY" in column headers.

Remuneration

Carefully consider the currency in which you will be paid and the location (country) where your pay will be deposited. A big part of this decision depends on your long-term goals, but be sure that you will be paid in a currency that retains its value in the country in which you intend to spend most of your time. It is best to be paid in a stable currency such as the German deutsche mark, the British pound, the United States dollar, or the Euro.

You will also want to ensure that your money remains accessible. For example, if a Canadian takes up residency in the United States, the Canadian is no longer allowed to change allocations or buy Canadian mutual funds contained within their Registered Retirement Savings Plan (similar to the U.S. 401k).

If expenses are part of your contract, you will want to ensure that they actually cover your cost of living. See Appendix B, "Per Diem Rates," for sample per diem rates from around the world.

Trial Period

A very good idea, once you are accepted for a foreign assignment, is to visit the country of assignment for a short period of time (e.g., a few weeks or a month) and then arrange your move. This option has several advantages. First, you will know after a few weeks if you can handle the assignment and whether you are interested in the contract. Many times the work that you will be doing is not the same as that which was advertised. A second advantage is that you will not have the extra burden of coordinating moving activities during your first few stressful weeks at the new contract. The cost to you will also be less if the client decides not to keep you. Finally, you will have the opportunity to explore and talk to the locals to learn such things as where to stay, how to apply to schools, and where to shop.

Making the Move

Listed below are some other points that will make a move to a new country easier and safer:

◆ Make sure that you have some cash available in your bank account. When arriving in a new country, there will be many small items that you will not have considered.

◆ Obtain good medical insurance before you leave. Also, consider a personal liability package and baggage insurance. Make sure that all policies are valid in the country that you are moving to.

◆ Make sure that your registered retirement funds (i.e., 401k or IRA) have their yearly maximum contributions contributed before you leave. Most countries will not allow you to contribute to your retirement fund if you are not a resident of that country.

◆ On arrival in the new country, make sure that you keep proof of your entry date. This can be as simple as obtaining a passport stamp or going down to the local authorities and registering yourself (registration is compulsory in some countries, such as Belgium and the Netherlands). This date is important for tax calculations and proof of residency.

Wrapping Up

International work can be fun and rewarding. You get the opportunity to travel around the world and get paid well to do it. There are several things to consider before packing your suitcase, however. You first must determine if you can handle overseas assignments. You must be able to work independently and handle all of the social and cultural changes that occur, in addition to working on a new contract.

If you decide that you are ready for locating the work, the most important points to consider are evaluating the different agencies, dealing with international taxes, paying relocation expenses, and obtaining a work visa. All of these things are not easy to do, but once completed, the rewards are there both monetarily and personally.

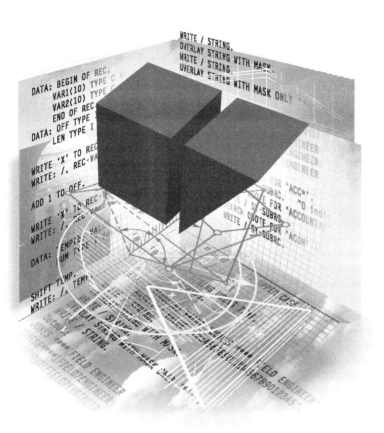

Chapter 7

Streamlining Operations

Your consulting work dominates your day. There is no reason to bring it home with you, unless you desire to do so. This chapter offers methods to organize your business so that the least amount of time is spent maintaining and running your consulting business.

The first step in simplifying your business life is obtaining the right equipment for your home and home office. In SAP consulting, it is impossible to survive without at least one computer and several types of communication capabilities.

Communications and Software

If your home base is close to where you consult, then a desktop computer makes more sense. However, if your home base is somewhere other than the area where you work, then a laptop computer is better suited to your needs. By using the docking stations that are available for laptops, you can have the convenience of a desktop on a laptop computer.

Table 7-1 lists some Web sites that are good sources of information about what computers are available.

Table 7-1 Online Sources for Computer Information

Web Site	Purpose
www.intel.com	Definitive guide of computer terms and explanation of new accessories.
www.yahoo.com	Enter '<PRODUCT NAME> review' as your search key words, and you will find out others' experiences with the product you are thinking of buying.
www.computers.com	A good resource for comparison shopping of systems and searching for particular features via the manufacturer.

As an SAP consultant, your computing needs will vary with your role in the SAP implementation (business consultant vs. developer). Just be sure that your computing

NOTE

The U.S. government encourages you to buy good equipment by permitting independent contractors and corporations to deduct from income capital expenses up to
$17,000 in capital goods. A way to look at the computer purchase is that the govern-
ment will pay for half of your computer purchase because you won't be taxed on the
money you spend on the computer. So, purchase what you need, and the government subsidizes your work-related capital goods.

capability satisfies your work needs. Besides specific SAP job-related tasks (e.g., logging on to SAP, viewing Microsoft Project), your new computer should have enough
computing power to organize your life, both logistically and financially.

 NOTE

Because the majority of computers in the corporate world are running under the
Microsoft banner, either on Windows 95/98 or a version of NT, our recommendations
pertain to the Windows operating system environment. Similar packages are available
for all other operating systems.

The three types of software that should be installed on your computer to make
you a more efficient and effective consultant are logistical organizational software,
financial organizational software, and the software that pertains to your specific
role in the SAP implementation.

Organizational Software

The first category of required software for the SAP consultant is the logistical
organization software. Lotus, Microsoft, and many other companies make a variety of software programs that combine e-mail, calendar, contact, and task management programs into one package. The benefit of such a software program is
that all of your information is centrally located. For example, you can read your
current e-mails and maintain this year's Christmas card list in the same program.
We use Outlook and then synchronize the software with a Personal Digital

Assistant (PDA) that we carry at all times. (PDAs are discussed later in this chapter, in "Personal Digital Assistants.")

With any software package, the first task is to bring the software online. This requires typing in all your contact information, as well as transferring your e-mail, faxes, appointments, and general notes. If you already use such a software package and all these pieces of information exist in separate programs, export the information from those programs in such a format that you can import it into your new software program.

NOTE

For more information on importing and other Outlook features, see Prima Tech's *The Essential Office 2000 Book.*

CAUTION

Always be sure to back up your original data files so that an accidental erasure of the data in the transfer process is not a catastrophic event.

Once the data is transferred to a program such as Outlook, use only that program to maintain that information. Once you centrally locate your information, you will become more effective and efficient at your tasks.

Personal Digital Assistants

A PDA is a small-scale computer that has at least 1 megabyte (MB) of RAM (Random Access Memory); some PDAs have as much as 16MB of RAM. The most convenient PDAs fit in a shirt pocket.

A PDA's primary purpose is organization, which is what you should be most concerned with. Regardless of which PDA you choose, make sure that it has synchronization capability with your organizational software. Most PDAs run on the latest Windows CE environment, which is compatible with Outlook.

The PDA allows you to take your information with you wherever you go. Generally, meetings are scheduled in other meetings or at someone's desk. Using a PDA, you can jot down notes, make appointments, write down contact information, or respond to e-mails without being in front of your computer. When you return to your computer, the PDA can synchronize its data with the data currently on your computer via a cable and a synchronization program. The benefit of the PDA is that your information is centrally located on your computer, but a second copy of it can travel with you as a backup.

Financial Software

The second category of software needed by an SAP consultant is financial organizational software such as Microsoft Money or Intuit Quicken. These two software programs are great to organize the home and automate finances and investments. If you are diligent in keeping the data in these programs current, then the trip to the accountant at tax time or when you need to make a big financial decision (marriage, home purchase, etc.) is an easy one. With a mouse click, you can print the reports the accountant needs.

Speak with your banking and investment account representatives about setting up your finances with this software. Most institutions now allow for online downloads of account information. Most online brokerage offices offer this feature as well. Loans are a little more complex to set up, but using a good book (see Prima Tech's *Organize Your Finances with Quicken 99 In a Weekend* or *Microsoft Money 99 Fast & Easy*), you should have no problem at all. If most of your accounts are downloadable, then maintenance becomes very easy.

TIP

An important part of the setup process is setting up the category section of a program such as Quicken. Categories are descriptions of where your money is being transferred to, spent on, or received from. You should customize the list to your particular spending habits.

Keep in mind that as you get busier, it might be worth your while to have a professional do your books, rather than trying to be a part-time accountant and a full-time SAP consultant. If you will be doing your own books for your business, have an accountant who is trained in QuickBooks, or the accounting software that you intend to use, set up your chart of accounts (configure your company file). Such

---

Quicken's Class Feature

An often-overlooked feature of Quicken is the class feature. For example, if you eat dinner out one night on a date with your significant other, and then another night you dine with a client, Quicken stores both items under the standard category "Dining." However, one should be reimbursed or written off, while the other should not be. To differentiate between these two expenses, associate a class to the business-related expense. When Quicken generates its reports of your expenditures, the personal expenses are separated from other expenses that are associated with classes. This is a good way to separate income streams or expenses, especially if you are working for several companies or are on several projects.

---

software tracks your timecards, as well as accounts receivable, accounts payable, and bank accounts. Use this software if you have business banking accounts and are billing your clients or agencies directly as an independent contractor or as a corporation. For more information, see Prima Tech's *Organize Your Business Finances with QuickBooks 99 In a Weekend.*

Consulting Tools

Finally, have a section of your computer dedicated to your development or consulting tools. Examples of these types of programs are Microsoft Visual Studio, SAP GUI interface, Cold Fusion, Microsoft Office, and Microsoft Project.

Essentially these are the tools that allow you to do your trade, which is to consult on SAP. The client should provide a system with which you can work, but you should always assume that you have to rely on yourself for all your resources.

Internet Accounts

SAP consultants need the capability to send and receive e-mail wherever they are in the world. Besides using your company's e-mail address, it is a good idea to maintain a static e-mail account where you can send and receive e-mail to and from colleagues, businesses, friends, and family.

E-mail Aliasing

A good way to keep your email address updated is to obtain an e-mail alias from a service. An alias is an e-mail address that points to your real e-mail address. For example, Gareth's e-mail alias is gmdebruyn@bigfoot.com, but his current real e-mail address is gmdebruyn@ix.netcom.com. In a few months, when he starts another project, his e-mail address might change, but rather than have his friends, colleagues, and family update their records, he just points the gmdebruyn@bigfoot.com to the new address. Think of this alias as a post office box that you give out as your address. You tell the company that maintains that post office box for you where you are located at all times. The company always forwards your mail to you. However, the people that need to remain in contact with you never see a disturbance in their records, because they always send their mail to the same place. The most popular and reliable ones right now are www.bigfoot.com and www.imail.com. Imail charges for certain domains, but Bigfoot is completely free. There are other forwarding services, but these two have been around for quite some time. Because the purpose of using an e-mail alias is to have a long-standing e-mail address, it makes sense to use one of the long-lasting services.

Another matter to consider is the actual connection to the Internet that allows you to surf the Web as well as get your e-mail. If you are traveling across time zones, it makes sense to use a service that is available nationwide. However, if you are living and working locally, using a local Internet service provider (ISP) makes sense if it offers you a good deal. See Prima Tech's *Get Your Family on the Internet In a Weekend* for more information.

Organizing Your Communication Systems

Next, you must organize the communication systems in your household. First and foremost, get a cell phone. Your clients or agents should be able to contact you no matter what, at any time. Also, at a client's site, a cell phone offers a discreet way to talk privately on the phone. If you are a private contractor or a corporation and use the cell phone primarily for business, then its cost is deductible.

At home, use your home telephone line for both business and personal use. Make sure your clients or employer knows that this number is your private home line, so that they do not abuse it. By giving them your cell phone number as well, they are able to leave you messages on your voicemail if you are not available. Of course, be sure to purchase the extra option plan when you get your cell phone. Most phones have options such as call forwarding, pager notification, and voicemail for a minimal extra cost.

Add to your home line a voicemail feature. If you are busy on a phone call, the calling party is forwarded to voicemail where they can leave a message rather than getting a continuous ringing or busy signal.

In addition to your home line, get a second line that is dedicated to modem and fax use. The clients who need to fax you have a number by which to do so. Also, when you log on to the Internet, download software upgrades, or connect remotely to client sites, your voice line is not tied up. If you are doing support work, it is essential that you be able to simultaneously log on to the R/3 system and walk someone through some steps over the phone.

Establishing Your Personal Support Team

Your job is SAP consulting, and you are the expert that a company brings in to do the job right. Likewise, you may sometimes need to act as an efficient company, and bring in to your life some experts to both simplify it and get the job done right. The goal of bringing on additional staff is to unburden yourself of work in a very cost-effective manner. The reason for having such a support team is that SAP implementations take a lot of time and energy. If this team is utilized, you will be able to maintain a successful personal and public lifestyle.

Financial Planner

Consider your financial planner to be the doctor you hopefully see only once a year. The financial planner does your yearly financial checkup. In addition to providing the level of guidance you need for your investments, it is their job to stay on top of the current tax laws. Depending on the level of service the planner provides, they can offer a list of tax ideas to present to your accountant in regards to the next tax season.

At minimum, have your financial planner do the following for you:

◆ Provide a list of realistic goals for the next year.

◆ Provide a current picture of your financial health.

◆ Provide some good suggestions for tax savings for the upcoming tax season.

◆ Analyze your retirement accounts and whether you are on track or not.

Lawyer

Lawyers are an essential part of your team when signing on to a new project. Do not sign a contract until your lawyer has reviewed it, despite the urging of your new employer, client, or agency. Your lawyer is your tool to reach your necessary level of satisfaction with the contract at-hand.

When dealing with your lawyer, be sure to spell out your future goals so that they can take them into account when reviewing the contract. If price is an issue for you, get your attorney to tell you how long it will take to review the contract and make the appropriate changes. At most, that time should not be more than a couple of hours.

Accountant

The same information that applies to your lawyer applies to your accountant. Be sure to meet with the accountant yearly to discuss your financial goals and your tax strategy for the upcoming season. An accountant makes doing your taxes much simpler by being aware of the current tax laws and applying them to your tax returns. They generally charge a flat fee for their services.

Comparing the Results

One year we compared the results from doing our taxes using tax preparation software to our accountant's results. Our accountant came up with a tax credit to us of a couple thousand dollars, while we came up with a tax debt of more than a couple thousand dollars. From that point on, we let him do his job, and paid him faithfully for his services.

An accountant is necessary when you are incorporated. It is a good practice to have your accountant give you a lesson on how to do your books and then review your books on a quarterly basis. Separate federal and state tax returns have to be filed for you and for your corporation.

Wrapping Up

SAP implementations are strenuous tasks that demand grueling schedules. By simplifying your life, you gain some free time to enjoy yourself and the company of friends and family. By having the right equipment and properly utilizing it, you become a more efficient and effective consultant. With a professional support staff, a financial planner, an accountant, and an attorney, you can be confident that your affairs will be kept in order.

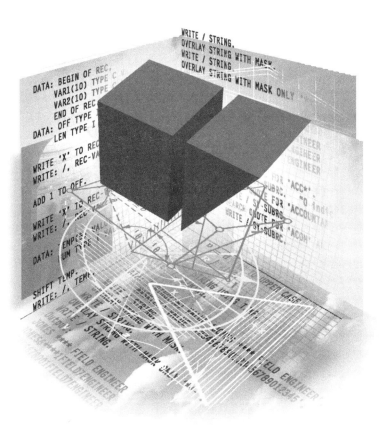

Chapter 8

Financial Planning

As a highly compensated SAP professional, whether as a contractor or as a permanent employee, you must manage your income wisely to save for the future and minimize your taxes. There are certain job expense and retirement strategies available to W-2 employees and for consultants who bill through their own private corporations.

Taxes

As an SAP consultant, you will earn a good deal of money, which will push you into the upper income tax brackets. There are certain steps that you can take to move yourself down the tax scale. This section discusses a few strategies that you can follow to reduce the amount of money you pay to the government each year. Use this section as the basis on which to make suggestions to your tax professional, accountant, or attorney. For tax rates, visit the IRS Web site (**www.irs.gov**).

Deferred Compensation Packages

Wouldn't it be nice to be able to instantly lower your tax liability by one tax bracket? Well, some companies offer that option through a deferred compensation package.

A deferred compensation package allows you to put money into a tax-free account that earns interest until you "claim" it. For example, if you make $150,000 per year, to lower your tax liability by one tax bracket, you must earn less than $100,000. By deferring your compensation, your company agrees to pay you $100,000 that year, thus lowering your tax bracket, and places the $50,000 balance into an account that you will claim later in the following years.

The goal is to effectively lower your income so that you pay less in taxes while still receiving your full compensation. High SAP salaries will not last forever, so if you are paid the money you earn now at a later date, you will be taxed at a lower bracket and make more money in the end. Effectively, you lose nothing because you are still allowed to invest the money that you have not claimed in certain investments. Be sure to speak to your tax professional or financial planner to make sure that the investments and plan are legitimate.

Retirement Plans

As an SAP consultant, it is likely that you exceed the limits for a Roth IRA, which are currently $95,000 if you are single and $150,000 if you are married, filing jointly. If you are earning less than this, consult an agent and get a new job.

Are you a W-2 wage earner or billing as an independent contractor through a corporation (a 1099 wage earner is treated the same as a corporation for retirement purposes). If you are a W-2 wage earner, then check whether your agency or consulting company offers a 401(k) plan. If you are contracting via 1099 or through your corporation, you qualify for a Keogh plan or an SEP IRA. As a W-2 employee, you may also have the opportunity of participating in a Keogh or SEP-IRA, but it depends on what the company you work for offers in the way of retirement plans.

401(k) Plans

Only W-2 employees qualify for a 401(k) plan. A 401(k) plan is a retirement savings plan that is used in place of a pension or profit-sharing plan. Essentially, the plan defers a portion of your compensation for retirement purposes. The current maximum tax-deferred employee contribution is $10,000. It is adjusted upward each year in accordance to the CPI (Consumer Price Index). The $10,000 is invested in funds selected by the company that administers the 401(k) plan for your company.

Some employers match your contributions to the 401(k) plan. This matching generally happens if you are a salaried SAP consultant working for a consulting company. If you are an hourly contractor working for an agency, you are probably making far too much money for the agency to match your contribution (their margin of earnings on your rates is smaller than that of a consulting firm).

This $10,000 is tax-deferred income. This means that it essentially is a $10,000 write-off for your taxes. Because W-2 consultants have very few write-offs, this is definitely one to take advantage of. We currently work for an agency, so we take advantage of this write-off. However, we also do 1099 work each year, which gives us the flexibility of also participating in another retirement plan, such as a Keogh or an SEP-IRA.

SEP-IRA

An SEP-IRA is reserved for employees of companies that offer the plan or self-employed individuals. Generally, self-employed individuals (1099 or S-corporations) utilize it.

 NOTE

If you employ other consultants through your company, these retirement plans become much more complicated. You must offer the same plan that you create for yourself to your employees, and you must contribute to their plans, matching their contributions. If you fall into this category, seek the guidance of a tax professional.

An SEP-IRA is very easy to set up, and the deduction allowed is much greater than that of a 401(k) plan. For tax years 1997 and 1998, the maximum contribution allowed was either 15 percent of adjusted gross 1099 income or $24,000, whichever was less.

The paperwork needed to set up an SEP-IRA is minimal. It's no more than is needed to open a regular contributory IRA. A broker or an investment company will give you the forms to start an SEP-IRA. Also, most investment companies have people dedicated to helping individuals and corporations set up the plan and become familiar with the rules governing them. An SEP-IRA can be opened for the tax year you are filing anytime before April 15th of the following year.

SIMPLE IRA

Another retirement plan option is the SIMPLE IRA. This plan is relatively new, set up for self-employed individuals (1099). The maximum contribution is $6,000 or the amount of money made through 1099 work. This plan is very simple to set up. Just fill out the forms with your broker and make the contribution for the applicable tax year. The account can be set up anytime before you file for that year (April 15th of the following year). This year we will be paid for this book through a 1099, paid for our consulting jobs via W-2s, and paid for some private consulting through our S-corporations. From our W-2 income, we contribute to our 401ks; from our book income, we contribute toward our SIMPLE IRAs; and from our private consulting, our S-corporations contribute to our SEP-IRAs.

This strategy allows us a great deal of deductions across the board, while building up retirement accounts for the future.

Contributory IRA

The most popular or well-known retirement plan is the contributory IRA. This plan allows for a $2000 contribution per tax year. While everyone is eligible to make this contribution to the retirement account, contributory IRA eligibility (for deduction) is even more stringent than that of the Roth IRA. Eligibility for a deduction begins to phase out for single taxpayers after $30,000 and for married taxpayers filing jointly after $50,000.

 NOTE

If you do not participate in an employer-sponsored retirement plan but your spouse does, eligibility phases out once your adjusted gross income exceeds $150,000. If neither of you participates in a company-sponsored retirement plan or if you are single and do not participate, then you are eligible for the $2000 contribution and deduction.

You might be tempted to make regular contributions to your contributory IRA each year for tax-deferred savings. Remember that when you withdraw this money during retirement, the gains that you have made on this account will be taxed at a personal income tax rate on the income from your retirement accounts.

If you plan wisely, this money will be much more than $100,000 per annum in today's dollars (just from 401(k) and other retirement accounts). The tax percentage will exceed 30 percent under today's tax schedule. However, if you take that same $2,000 and invest it in stock or mutual funds that you hold long-term, your long-term capital gains rates will be only 20 percent at today's tax rates. Another option is to take that $2,000 and invest it in tax-free municipal bonds, which yield about six to eight percent per annum and are tax free.

Keogh Plan

Another option for retirement is the Keogh, or HR-10, plan. This plan is very similar to a SEP-IRA, but it requires significantly greater administration effort and is for self-employed individuals. Also, once you commit to this plan, you must contribute the same percentage each year. You can contribute from three percent to twenty-five percent each year to a maximum of $30,000. The Keogh plan must be set up in the tax year that it will be applied. Contributions can be made until April 15th of the following year.

Retirement Plan Advantages

Retirement plans offer two advantages. First, there is the possibility of a tax deduction. Second, your retirement accounts can grow as tax deferred savings, thus growing at a much faster rate than your regular investment or savings accounts.

Per Diems

Per diem is the term that describes what a W-2 employee receives in reparation for expenses incurred in traveling to and from and working at a client's site. The per diem should cover your food, travel, and lodging expenses. The IRS has rules that govern per diem rates. A current copy of the maximum rates allowed to be paid, ordered by city, is found on the IRS Web site (**www.irs.gov**). Per diems are not reported on your W-4 statement at the end of the year as income. Discuss with your accountant how to handle the per diem income. Sometimes you will be paid a per diem that is more than you can spend. By current rules, you should pay taxes on the difference.

After one year in an assignment, per diems are no longer allowed, at least for W-2 employees. The IRS feels that if you work at a client's site for over a year, then you are no longer traveling to that site, but rather that is where you reside. So, per diems can no longer be paid to you without you paying taxes on the income (at least as a W-2 employee).

Per diems are easily handled by 1099 contractors or consultants who bill through a corporation. Any business expenses that you incur outside of your rate are billed to your client and then paid back to you.

Handling Expenses

Save all your tax-related receipts for your SAP jobs. At the end of each month, balance your files and allocate those expenses to your jobs. Then, at the end of the year, print out your lists of where all your money went, subdivided by your SAP consulting practices. Your accountant then finds it very easy to take those amounts and itemize them into your taxes.

As for other expenses such as food and travel, the same principle applies. Organize an expense report at the end of each month and staple those receipts along with descriptions of how you spent the money to the expense reports.

Strategies for W-2 Employees

As a W-2 employee, you are fairly restricted in your tax deduction strategy. The best tax deduction currently is a mortgage. You can write off any interest that you pay on that mortgage. Additional write-offs that you should pursue are any educational courses (retraining that doesn't move you out of your current career) and your 401(k) plan. The best strategy we have found as W-2 employees is to make a little 1099 income and lose a great deal of money against that 1099 income. For example, make $5,000 in 1099 income and lose $10,000 against that income, which results in a $5,000 loss against your W-2 income. Another federal deduction that many people forget is your state tax. Any money that you pay to your state as income tax is an instant write-off when you itemize.

TIP

Hire a professional tax accountant! The $300 you will pay the accountant will be reimbursed by what you save in taxes paid.

Strategies for 1099 Contractors

Any 1099 income is considered business income. Businesses have a great deal of latitude in writing off items on taxes. Any capital expenses up to $17,000 (computer, fax machine, personal digital assistant, cell phones, etc.) are fully deductible if used for business purposes. Any capital expenses over $17,000 are depreciable over five years, which means that each year you can take a certain percentage of that item as a tax deduction.

In addition to capital expenses, any service-related expenses that you incur are deductible. Your online Internet service provider fees and cell phone bill are deductible, as long as you use them exclusively for business purposes.

Also, as a 1099 contractor, you have the flexibility of opening a Keogh, SEP-IRA, or SIMPLE IRA as a retirement plan, which is a great tax deduction.

Strategies for Corporations

As a corporation, you have all the deductions that a 1099 has, plus more. A corporation is a separate entity from its stockholders and can conduct business transactions on its own. For instance, your corporation can lease a car and write it off as a business expense.

Child Employment

Because you are already paying money to your child in the form of expenses, employ the child and write the money off. Up to $4,250 is tax free to your child, as a tax deduction to you. When your child reaches the age of 14, the child is allowed to participate in the contributory IRA program, so if you pay the child $6,250, they can put $2,000 into an IRA as a deduction and pay no tax on the remaining $4,250.

A more complex strategy is to donate $10,000 worth of capital goods towards your child's trust. First, your corporation has already claimed that $10,000 worth of capital goods as a business deduction, so that is your first tax write-off. Second, once your child's trust has that $10,000, lease the equipment back to the corporation (phones, computers, etc.). The leasing fees are tax deductible to the corporation. And as long as the income to the trust is below a certain amount, the trust will be taxed at a very minimal rate, if at all.

A corporation has its own tax ID number. A good way to keep track of expenses is to sign up for an American Express Corporate Card. Then charge all your business expenses to this card. At the end of the year, you have a complete record of most of your business expenses.

Business Expenses

If you use your computer for SAP consulting or tracking your investments, the percentage of time used for this purpose can be multiplied against the cost of the computer and it can be written off.

Another expense that you can write off is if you use a room in your house exclusively for business purposes. However, this write-off is exclusive to 1099 and corporation income only. W-2 employees cannot write off this expense. In addition to the square footage of the room, you can write off a certain percentage of utilities as they relate to this room. In the simplest terms, the rules state that you must exclusively use this room for business purposes. So, make sure that this room has its own lock, has a separate phone line, and that you only do business (computer work, consulting, etc.) there. Basically, what the government is telling you is that if you use a spare room in your house for business purposes exclusively, it will pay for half the expense for that room (you don't pay taxes on that amount of money). By turning regular expenses into business expenses, you create deductions against your regular income, which will lower your overall taxes.

Insurance

If you are a permanent employee, some insurance will be provided as part of your compensation.

Health

Are you single or married? Do you have any children? If you are single without children, then health insurance is a very affordable benefit. Affordable health insurance for such an individual currently costs around $60 a month through an employer. However, for a married individual with children, full medical insurance can cost up to $500 a month.

As a permanent employee, health and dental insurance are necessary. If you are a consultant who is going through an agency or a private contractor billing through your corporation, you will need to purchase your own health and dental insurance. As a consultant billing through an agency, see if the agency will pay your health insurance on a pre-tax basis. This way the agency pays your health insurance with pre-tax dollars, and you are only taxed on the remainder. Essentially, the government pays half of your health insurance.

If you are billing your client through your corporation, then have your corporation buy the health insurance for you. The corporation can buy the health insurance and write it off as a business expense.

Dental Insurance?

How does a corporation or a permanent employee handle dental insurance? Well, unless you have some major dental problems, we would recommend just finding a good dentist and paying for the cleanings (and fillings?) out of pocket. We have found that dental insurance is a very complex thing, and after getting it, and then visiting the dentist and finding out what the dental insurance will and will not pay for, it is not worth the headache and the money for the insurance.

Automobile

As a highly compensated individual, it behooves you to get full liability insurance for your automobile. If you have an accident that is your fault, the court will have no problem billing you for the expenses of the other party. All in all, auto insurance is not that expensive if you shop around, and it's required in many states. Also, if you get homeowner's insurance and auto insurance from the same agent, you should get a significant discount.

Life

Do you have dependents? If you do not, then you should get life insurance that only covers your current liabilities or term life insurance. Other policies don't expire, but act like a savings account as well as a life insurance policy. These policies cost more, and it may be more beneficial to you to take the difference between the term life insurance policy premium and the savings life insurance premium and invest that difference in a private account.

If you have a family who is dependent on you and your salary, you want to make sure that they are not left stranded if something drastic happens. First and foremost, you want to take care of your liabilities (home, credit cards, etc.). Second, you want to provide a stable income for your family so that they can survive. Although this reason might require a second insurance policy until you can save enough money to provide for that, it is best that you start that savings now because it will grow faster than you think, eliminating the need for this second policy. For the first reason (to cover liabilities), pick an amount and term that covers your debts. For instance, if you have a 30-year mortgage and you owe $150,000, then perhaps get an $80,000 policy, which would pay for the mortgage payments first, and the interest would provide enough income to pay the mortgage payments until the thirtieth year.

If you are a permanent employee and your company offers this benefit, take it. Some companies offer such a benefit for an extremely reasonable price.

Saving and Investing

As an SAP professional, you are in a desirable field. Just like lawyers in the 1980s and emergency room doctors in the 1990s, people are now flocking to the computer industry because it is a highly lucrative field. As an SAP professional, you must create a financial security blanket for yourself. This especially applies to contractors because the consulting company is not training you in new skills. You are doing that on your own, and at the same time you must stash away cash for lean times. You should become, in effect, your own financial manager, saving money now so that later in life you can enjoy it without worry. By saving now, you take away most of the risk that being a contractor offers.

When we first started consulting (contracting in our case), the first things that we did were to pay off our outstanding liabilities (credit cards) and create a savings fund. Once we had that security fund built up, we started to overflow the money into accounts that we'd use for future investing, for such things as a home, retirement, and our children's college.

If you live beneath your means as an SAP consultant, and save the rest for a rainy day, you will be very surprised at how fast your savings and peace of mind will grow. The key to becoming your own financial manager is to start good habits early. Figure out how much you need to live. Increase that by 15 percent so that you have some play money. Then take the rest of the money and just transfer it to an investment account where you or a professional broker or investment manager makes it grow.

Pay Yourself First

There is an old financial rule that states that you should live within your means, no matter whether you're a millionaire or a street sweeper. Your goal is to live a little

---

Paying Your Personal Bill

At minimum, you should save 10 percent of your income. If you earn $120,000 per year, you would pay yourself $1,000 each month, just like a bill, into a savings account of your choice (e.g., a brokerage account, a certificate of deposit, or regular savings).

This method of paying a percentage of your paycheck each time you receive one is called paying yourself first. Essentially it is just a good habit to establish so that you save on a regular basis. For some reason, paying oneself first emulates paying a bill, which makes it easier to save on a regular basis. Also, if you pay your savings before you let a surplus build in an account, it is much less likely that you will spend that money frivolously.

---

better than that street sweeper, and save the rest of your money so later in life you become a millionaire.

A simple concept that will allow you to achieve this goal (living beneath your means) is to pay yourself first. Consider your savings to be another bill, just like a car payment. If at the beginning of the month you pay your utilities, your car loan, your mortgage, and a specific amount to a savings account that you cannot touch, you will be left with a certain amount of money to live on. You will find that if you follow this regimen, your savings will grow very quickly (especially if it is in an account that you will not take money from).

Saving for Lean Times

First, determine what you need as income to survive on a monthly basis. Add up all your liabilities (loans), your nondiscretionary expenses (rent, car insurance, etc.), and your discretionary expenses (dining out, telephone calls, clothing allowance, cash). Calculate all these costs on a monthly basis, and practice sticking to this budget. Be sure to file away the budget because if you are ever laid off work, it will be your game plan.

For lean times, our rule of thumb is that we will have enough cash to pay for 12 months of mortgage payments and 6 months of no work whatsoever.

Online Brokerage Accounts

As an SAP professional, most of your time will be spent at work. If you wish to be actively involved in how your savings money is invested, then open an account with an online brokerage house and trade over the World Wide Web.

Otherwise, just defer to a professional, such as a full service broker. However, most people in technology like to dabble in the stock market, especially as technology stocks are very much on the move right now.

If you plan to open an online account, then you should find out who the reputable online trading brokerages are. Keep in mind that certain online brokerage shops are new and potentially less reliable, so be sure to pick a reputable service.

Wrapping Up

Currently, the United States Congress is considering a bill to implement personal finance as a required course in high schools across the United States. As an SAP professional, this is a required course if you wish to survive. While the SAP market is very hot, it is essential that you save for the future. There are several strategies to implement. First, minimize your tax bill. Second, put money into your retirement accounts. Third, spend your money wisely and save for the future. This portion of the job can be a fun one, or it can be a burden. If you follow some of the tips in this chapter and are realistic about your lifestyle, you can make this part of SAP consulting a very positive one. Remember to take full advantage of the existing laws and regulations to pay the minimum legal tax.

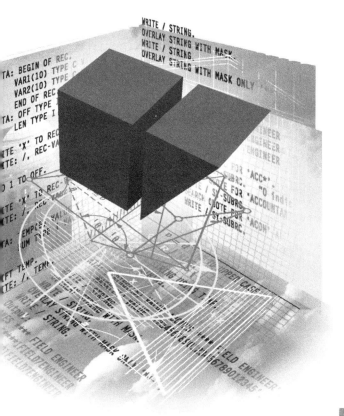

PART II

The SAP Work Environment

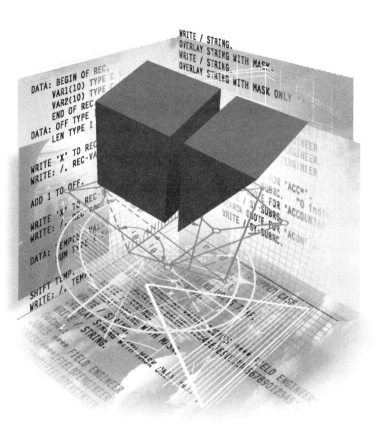

Chapter 9

Your First Week

The first week of any contract is critical; clients form their impressions of you during this time. This is especially true for SAP contracts because clients usually have very high expectations for SAP consultants. Developing a solid working relationship with the customer requires an understanding of the client and getting up to speed quickly.

Making a Good First Impression

Whether you are a permanent employee switching organizations or a consultant at a new client site, you must make a good first impression. It's easier to do than trying to change peoples' minds about you if you leave a bad first impression.

Your First Meeting

During your first meeting (or your first few days) at the client's site, you will learn exactly what your task is. It is very important to get to know each person you meet and understand where that person fits in either the consulting or client organization. Also, you should review preliminary documentation that pertains to the project prior to any meeting so that you have some idea of what the project is about.

During the meeting, it is more important to listen than to talk, and to only ask questions that specifically relate to what you have been contracted for. If you are assigned any action items during the meeting, before the meeting ends, make sure that you know who to go to for more details, clarification, or assistance.

To design a solution, you should understand the problem. If you have only been on the project for a day or so, do not offer any solutions until you completely understand the needs of the client. This demonstrates honesty and indicates that you don't rush to solutions that are not well thought-out.

Your First Walk through the Office

Usually you will have a tour of the office during your first day on the job. You will be introduced to many people. It is important to identify the project consultants and who will be able to help you through the first few weeks. Concentrate on remembering these people (having an organization chart in-hand will help) and then broaden your relationships as time goes on. Always be sure you introduce yourself to people in a friendly manner that leaves other consultants and clients knowing that they can come to you with questions or information. You never know which relationships will be of greatest benefit to you, so don't close the doors on any!

Pecking Order Among the Consultants

Consultants on a project all have varying degrees of experience and knowledge of SAP. To find out, begin asking questions of everyone, and it will become apparent who knows what. There is no single person who understands everything in SAP, and consultants tend to specialize in different areas.

This pecking order works both ways. When you go to a new SAP site, people may come to you asking questions. Your answers will determine where they place you on the contractor "knowledge hierarchy" list. Work especially hard on answering questions during the first few weeks. When someone asks you a question, make sure you understand specifically what they want, and then if you do not know the answer, say that you will get back to them later. Ensure that you do get back to people on all questions asked (even if the answer is that you do not know or could not find out the answer).

Keys for Good First Impressions

Here are some ways to ensure that you make a good first impression:

◆ **Arrive on time.** Never be late for a scheduled appointment. If you're delayed, be sure to call before your appointment.

◆ **Talk less, listen more.** Control the conversation by asking questions, but do not monopolize it. It's just as important to listen. If you are unsure of what is being discussed, ask questions for clarification, or rephrase a statement in your own words for the purpose of understanding it. Be careful to keep emotion out of rephrasing—you should not be offering opinions at this time.

◆ **Don't offer solutions before you know what the need is.** Ask about the the needs and wants before making recommendations.

◆ **Treat the receptionist and secretary with respect.** These are the people who understand office chemistry and structure and who can make your life easier or more difficult—depending on their first impression of you.

◆ **Use appropriate language.** Do not use slang or words such as "yeah." Try to sound as educated as possible when you speak.

◆ **Have a positive attitude.** Always smile and remember to ooze an upbeat, positive vibe.

◆ **Dress appropriately for the client's site.** Try to find out the appropriate attire before you arrive at the client's site. If it is a suite office, find out if they are conservative or modern, but lean toward conservative for your first day. If office dress is casual, go in business casual. Never dress more casually than your client dresses.

Make Your Client and Peers Look Good

When starting a contract, it is important to avoid grandstanding about how you can or will solve all of the problems that others could not. Also, do not criticize work already done by others. During the first few weeks, you do not have enough knowledge about the complexities or history of a certain solution to say that it can be done easily or that it should have been done a different way. Instead, give credit to others for getting as far as they have.

Remember that both technical needs and intracompany politics drive SAP projects. Sometimes the technically correct solution is overturned for a less viable option just to meet some intracompany political agenda.

Expectations of an SAP Consultant

Clients have higher expectations for SAP consultants than for other types of consultants and contractors. These higher expectations are driven by many factors and usually translate into higher compensation. An effective SAP consultant provides a more comprehensive knowledge base and a higher dedication level than is usual among consultants.

The primary reason for this is that SAP is an Enterprise Business Solution, which provides a suite of software applications fully integrated into one environment.

> ## An Early Exit
>
> A client commonly uses several consultants in the early stages of a project and then lets natural selection determine which to keep. The client considers each consultant's ability to contribute to the project and then lets the weaker consultants go after a few weeks. We have been at sites where two ABAP consultants were hired, but after one week, one was let go because only one position was available. Of course, the two consultants were never informed that they were competing for one job. If you are let go after a short tenure, do not consider it a failure, but do insist on an exit interview to ensure that you improve on any mistakes that you may have made.

Because programs, solutions, and customizations used in one area can easily affect those used in other areas, an effective consultant has at least some basic business knowledge of many SAP areas, and is willing to invest the time to learn as much about the client's environment as possible.

Because of its integrated nature and extensive functionality, SAP is not a simple system to learn. Many veteran SAP individuals say, "Every time I learn another area of SAP, I realize there is more to learn."

SAP implementations are usually quite large and delays can quickly add up to millions of dollars. If a client hires a Java programmer and finds out that the programmer is not that quick, it may be forgiven; but this is not acceptable for an SAP consultant. The client is paying top dollar and demands the best.

The SAP Team Atmosphere

SAP originated in Germany more than 20 years ago and today has an installed base worldwide. SAP established sales offices in major cities around the world, with consultants from these offices assisting customers with installations. Walldorf, Germany, is still the primary development location for SAP, although there are now development centers in other parts of the world. It's easy to understand why many senior SAP consultants on projects in the United States are from Europe.

When you arrive on a project, you are likely to meet people from another part of the world. Besides a possible language difference, there are cultural differences. This environment requires extra effort on your part to ensure that you can work with all members of the team, which is critical for your project's success and for your contribution to it. Because you cannot change a company's culture, it is in your best interests to adapt to that culture as quickly as possible while remaining professional and polite.

When you first arrive at a client's site, assume that the other consultants are more experienced than you and probably know what they are talking about. After a few weeks, when you are accustomed to the project, analyze their ideas and, when you are ready, open a dialog with them to better understand why they have come to the realizations that they have.

Company Culture

Each company has its own culture. A company's culture defines its communications style, how it gets things done, how its people interact, and how its people make decisions. It is very important during the first week or so to get a good reading of your new client's culture. Then prepare yourself to adapt to that culture so it increases your effectiveness.

One of the most important cultural aspects of the company is the decision-making process. Is the process more like a democracy or a dictatorship? The answer helps determine how and to whom to sell your ideas. If your client is more like a democracy, then you must develop ground roots support for your ideas by discussing your ideas with many people and getting their feedback and approval before trying to implement them. In a company that is run more like a dictatorship, you must sell your ideas to a select group of people who have the trust of the leader and without whose support your ideas will go nowhere. It is also important in a dictatorship-style organization not to go against decisions that have already been made; in a democracy, such entrepreneurship is better tolerated

How companies treat consultants is also important. Some companies treat consultants as they treat their employees, while other companies have a separate set of rules for consultants. When starting a contract, never assume that you are invited to a meeting just because the rest of your group is going, or that you are allowed to participate in afterwork functions. Always ask whether you can or should attend.

Be wary of adopting traits of the company culture that inhibit the decision-making process and your contributions. An example of this is an organization that may have many meetings where not very much is accomplished. In this case, you should try to bow out of any meeting that you feel will not be informative or not allow you to participate and contribute as you should.

No More Starting from Scratch

The client starts from scratch on many non-SAP IT (Information Technology) projects. Databases and relationships must be defined, integration into other company modules must be specified, user interfaces designed, and so on. This is definitely not the case with SAP projects. SAP has been successfully implemented in thousands of companies. There are very few occasions where SAP cannot be configured or slightly modified to completely meet a client's needs.

An SAP consultant must learn as much as possible about setting up SAP in a variety of environments, including the following:

- **Learning an application rather than developing a solution from scratch.** Because most IT projects are in-house or custom development projects, this is the process that many IT professionals are familiar with. With a package installation, you skip some of the traditional IT design and development phases in the project, but other steps become even more important. An analysis of the client's business needs is critical because the implementation of these needs requires that the SAP consultant understand the countless variations and variables on how to make SAP do what the customer wants.

- **Finding detailed documentation for a specific behavior or functionality.** This is still a challenge because most of the system's source code is documented in German, and much of the Customization documentation has very little detail. Although there is more and more documentation being released all the time, it may still not be what you require. Because there are not many off-the-shelf books available on the various application modules in SAP, you will need access to SAP documentation.

◆ **Keeping abreast of the latest technology that SAP provides.** Every few years, SAP updates its hardware. The applications and development environment are continuously enhanced and improved upon. It is likely that no two consecutive projects you work on will utilize the same SAP release. For some technical folks, there is also the added variable of the database and operating system on which SAP operates. To be as flexible as possible for your future clients, you must learn to navigate in SAP and find what you are looking for in a variety of ways. Don't hardwire yourself to a particular menu path or transaction. Learn about its relationship to other functions in the system, so that when you work on a different release, finding what you need is easier and less time-consuming.

Standards and Naming Conventions

Every company has its own way of doing business, and this requires standards and naming conventions. In some organizations these are well-defined, while in others there may be none. Do not assume that two organizations are alike, even if they are part of the same company.

Existing Standards

When starting at a new organization, it is very important to become part of the implementation team, and to be able to adjust to the team's way of doing things quickly. One of the most obvious ways to work as an effective team member is to adopt the team's operation standards (whether they be development standards, requirements definition forms, issue documentation procedures, or something else). The first step is to find out what standards the company has in place. Standards can be as simple as naming conventions used in ABAP programming or as complicated as procedures to follow for laying out the business requirements and resulting configuration for an SAP module. If standards do not exist in the area of your contribution, you can suggest the need for them or propose such standards yourself—if you have the experience to do so.

Consider that companies that implement SAP now will probably still be running SAP in 20 years. Standards are developed so that everyone works in the same fashion, whether this is a new implementation or support work for an existing implementation. With ABAP standards, for example, all programs are structured the same way. This enables the programmer familiar with the standards to troubleshoot efficiently because they know where certain modules are, where and how variables are declared, and how the file I/O (input/output) should work.

Documentation standards ensure that each project has its documentation in the same format so that if someone needs to look something up, they know how to do so. During a project, a great deal of business knowledge is gathered and used to set up various configurations and specifications for programs. If the business needs or goals change, the ability to quickly review the reasons behind the original solutions is very valuable and helps ensure that some critical function is not lost due to changes.

From a consultant's viewpoint, the most important aspect of standards is that they remain consistent. You may know of a better way to produce documentation and do project plans or layout programs or training outlines, but unless there is a compelling reason to switch from the company's existing standard, it is best to stick with it. It is okay to expand on a standard when it is obvious that there are missing components. But a total switch is very expensive and should be avoided. Another important aspect of the standards is the ability to access the resulting information.

It is possible that your client has decided to adopt the practices and standards of a big consulting firm. In this case, you would need to adopt those standards as well. Most clients who partner with a big firm do so for the benefit of the project management practices and standards that the big firm developed. The big firm often provides a client with a step-by-step approach to implementing an application such as SAP, which can have a very different implementation life-cycle than an in-house-developed application. If the consulting partner has published a set

---

Coordinating Interfaces

We were involved in a contract where the client had adopted the use of a code generator for writing interfaces. This particular code generator had many shortfalls, and it was fairly easy to demonstrate that any interface could be coded from scratch faster and more efficiently than by using the generator. However, because all of the existing interfaces were written using the code generator, the new interfaces we designed also used the code generator. It was very important that all of the interfaces be set up and operate in the same fashion.

of standards on how it implements projects, it is in your best interests to learn and adopt these standards. Deviating from its format may hurt you at the current project, and may hinder your chances of getting on a project with the same consulting partner later.

Default Standards

If there are no existing standards to go by, either from the client or from the consulting group running the project, then you should at least try to implement some standards in your area.

One approach to developing standards (or to enhancing ones that are already in place) is to adopt SAP standards. Accelerated SAP (ASAP) provides an implementation methodology that takes a project through all its phases, including:

- **Project Preparation**. The project's scope, initial budgets, schedules, technical infrastructure, implementation strategies, and team definition are defined in this phase.

- **Business Blueprint**. The customer's business goals are defined and made understandable in this phase. Also, the business processes required to support these goals are identified.

- **Simulation**. During this phase, the SAP system is configured and enhanced to meet the business goals outlined in the previous steps. In this stage of the project, customer involvement is usually low.

- **Validation**. In this phase, solutions developed in the simulations phase evolve into an integrated and documented package that fulfills the customer's business goals. During this phase, customer involvement is quite high.

- **Final Preparation**. Final system testing is performed and end-users are trained during this phase. Data is also ported over along with the solution to the production environment.

- **Going Live and Support**. After its implementation, the system is reviewed to ensure that the business goals are fully met. Also included in this phase is the support of ongoing process improvements.

If the project you are working on does not subscribe to ASAP, the implementation guide (a subset of ASAP) also provides basic rules to adopt when implementing a project. SAP also includes standards for programming in its online help.

Asking the Right Questions

Don't ask questions that anyone with even a limited amount of knowledge of the subject should know. Whether a question should or shouldn't be asked depends on what the question is, when it is asked, and of whom it is asked.

It is not bad to ask questions when you are new to a client site. As an SAP consultant or a permanent employee in a new division, your time is very valuable to the company, and any time you save by asking someone questions rather than figuring out the answers yourself is beneficial. Of course, you have to be careful of whom you ask the questions; asking the top consultants to answer questions that anyone could answer is not a good idea.

These questions need to be answered for most types of SAP consulting work:

- ◆ **What is the system environment's composition?** An SAP consultant needs to know the logons for client intranet office systems, SAP clients, SAP system names, clients, and the general hardware architecture (if determined). Find out right away who to ask about the system environment, user IDs, passwords, and so forth, and then find that person!

- ◆ **What is each SAP client's purpose?** Either your project contact or the environment owner should be able to answer these questions for you. Find out where customizations should be done, where master data can or cannot be changed, and where transactional data can be entered.

- ◆ **Who do I go to for security profile issues and other technical problems?**

- ◆ **How do I transport code and customizations, and who approves them?**

- ◆ **How often is the development environment refreshed with production data (if at all), and are any special steps needed?**

- ◆ **What types of office software packages are used, and where should documents be stored?** Ask this question of a client contact at a peer level with you; don't ask the project manager.

- ◆ **What special industry-specific terminology (and other industry-related questions) do I need to know?** Although you may have extensive knowledge in SAP, you may not be familiar with the terminology or other industry-specific matters.

When Not to Ask Questions

Generally, it is not a good idea to ask questions during a meeting unless you feel that you must understand something immediately. Simply make a note of the question and then ask someone about it later. You may, at the end of a meeting, say that you have a number of questions about a specific topic and then ask whom best to discuss these questions with.

When to Ask Questions

If you do not understand why a client has decided to do something in a particular fashion, the first few weeks are an excellent time to ask such a question. This shows that you already understand something about how the client has set something up and that you have some knowledge about the subject. There usually is a good reason for the way things are set up, and when you get the answer to your question, you will also learn some more about the client's business and proposed solution. Of course, depending on where your client is in the implementation life cycle, any change of approach that you might suggest may not be appropriate.

Acronyms

One of the most frustrating things for us at a new contract site is figuring out what everyone is talking about. Each company has its own language and uses acronyms extensively. SAP also has its own set of acronyms, but this is used at all SAP sites.

Common Acronyms Used at a Client Site

During your first few days, you must resist the urge to interrupt every conversation for an explanation of all the acronyms as they are used. What we do is ask about an acronym if it is vital to comprehend an important conversation. We also ask about an acronym if we hear it mentioned many times. Otherwise, we just keep a list of the acronyms and then ask someone about them in one shot.

Common Acronyms Used in SAP

Just like clients, SAP has its own set of acronyms. Table 9-1 lists acronyms that are commonly used in the SAP world.

Table 9-1 Common Acronyms Used in SAP

Acronym	Meaning
ABAP	Advanced Business Application Programming
ALE	Application Link Enabling
AM	Fixed Asset Management Module
ARICE	Authorizations, Reports, Interfaces, Conversions, and Enhancements
ASAP	Accelerated SAP implementation
ATP	Available to Promise
BAPI	Business Application Programming Interface
BDC	Batch Data Communications
BOM	Bill of Material
BOR	Business Object Repository
CATT	Computer-Aided Test Tool
CO	Controlling Module
CPI	Common Programming Interface
CPI-C	Common Programming Interface–Communication
CUA	Common User Access
EAN	International Article Number
EDI	Electronic Data Interchange
EPC	Event-Driven Process Chain
FI	Finance Module
GUI	Graphical User Interface
HR	Human Resource Module
ICC	Interclient Communications
IDES	International Demonstration and Education System
IDOC	Intermediate Document
IMG	Implementation Guide
ITS	Internet Transaction Server
MM	Material Management Module
MPS	Master Production Scheduling
MRP	Material Requirements Planning
NFS	Network File System
OAG	Open Application Group
OC	Office and Communications
OTF	Output Text Format

Table 9-1 Common Acronyms Used in SAP *(continued)*

Acronym	Meaning
PAI	Process After Input
PBO	Process Before Output
PI	Physical Inventory
PM	Plant Maintenance Module
PP	Production Planning
PS	Project System Module
QAPI	Queue Application Programming Interface
QM	Quality Management Module
REO	Reorganization Data
RFC	Remote Function Call
RFQ	Request for Quotation
RPC	Remote Procedure Call
SD	Sales and Distribution
SNA	Systems Network Architecture
WBS	Workbreakdown Structure
WF	Workflow

Wrapping Up

To develop a strong foundation for a future working relationship, consultants must understand the expectations of their clients, what drives these expectations, and how to meet these expectations. SAP consulting is different from other types of consulting, and this is reflected in the compensation and the expected knowledge level of the consultants. First impressions are essential to developing working relationships with both the client and other consultants on a project.

Your first few days are full of new contacts, meetings, questions, and buzzwords, all of which must be dealt with properly to build good impressions about you in the minds of other people. Making a good first impression is the key to developing good working relationships with both the client and the other project consultants.

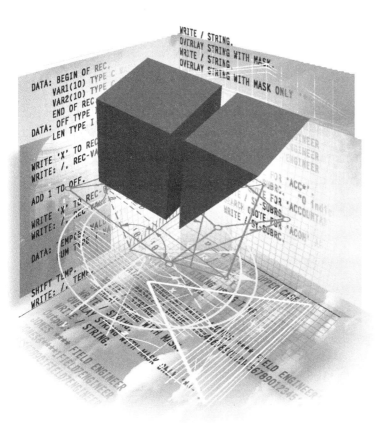

Chapter 10

Your Last Week

The work that you perform and your interaction with colleagues during a contract's last week are important. People you worked with during this contract may be future references or this client may have future work for you. The last week of work at a client site means wrapping up any outstanding work, ensuring that all documentation is complete, and transferring information to your colleagues.

In an ideal situation, you have set up all your documentation so that the client can easily find things. Additionally, the client will have the resources in place to take over any ongoing tasks that you were responsible for.

During the last week, go through your work area to make sure that nothing private is left behind and that all client reference material finds a home. Go through your workstation's hard drive to ensure that there are no critical or private documents on it.

Do not leave a client's site without giving the client a way to get in touch with you. It is wise to leave the client with the impression that you care about its operations.

Ongoing Support Contracts

When leaving a client's site at the end of a contract, you are not just physically leaving; you are also taking a considerable amount of knowledge about your work. Even with the best knowledge transfer, there are many details that only you know or understand. A client's comfort with this depends on the nature of your work and the thoroughness of the knowledge transfer. Many clients understand the risks but are still willing to undertake support themselves. Other clients, however, are somewhat nervous about providing support themselves, especially if they do not have adequate replacement staff or if the work that you were doing was very important. Ongoing support contracts help ease such clients' concerns during the period before your departure since they know that if they get in a real bind, they can still get your services.

The support contract benefits you and the client because it outlines the details of the support you will provide after you have finished a contract, including the level of support and how promptly this support will be provided. This limits the calls from a prior client while you are at a new contract. The support contract also places a monetary value on your time.

Charging Old Clients

Charging old clients has two purposes: to provide compensation for the work that you perform and to make the old client aware that it has to pay for your services.

This said, you also do not want to charge old clients for every five-minute phone call. It can be a nice break to get a call from your old workplace and to offer the old client quick, helpful advice. However, if the calls are frequent (more than once per week) or if the answers require more than a few minutes of your time, you must either say that you cannot help them or start charging for your services. If there is no service contract in place, let the client know that you would love to help but that it would take a few hours of your time, and without a contract, you cannot do anything for them.

Creating an Ongoing Support Contract

Ongoing support contracts can be created just before you leave a contract or after you have left. When your contract is nearly expired and you know that you will not sign an extension, you should make a judgment call about the likelihood of the client relying on your support after you leave. This reliance may not be continuous; it may be only for critical situations.

For example, if you are the only ABAP (Advanced Business Application Programming) developer of a complicated order-processing SAP bolt-on or a large financial interface, the client may only need your support if there is a problem. Only if it is obvious that the client will require your support should you approach the client about a support contract.

If you do not have a support contract in place and you find that an old client is relying on you to provide them with support, it is time to set up the contract. How complicated this is depends to a great extent on your current work arrangements, including whether you are working for the agency that originally set you up with this client and whether you have the time to provide the support that the client needs.

Support contracts are different than regular contracts. A support contract has to contain most of the details of a regular contract and must also outline the amount and timeliness of the support work.

All support contracts should contain the following sections:

♦ **Compensation.** Compensation is the rate at which you will be paid for the work you will do. This rate should not be greater than your rate when you left the client. The contract should also outline how, when, and who will pay you. Depending on the situation, you may also want to include a clause that specifies a different rate for holiday work. Other areas to cover are expenses such as long distance telephone charges and travel.

♦ **Duration of Contract.** This clause outlines how long the contract will be in effect.

♦ **Response Time.** This clause outlines how fast you will respond to a call and may specifically outline the times when you will not be available. Depending on the situation, you may want to have separate clauses for different response times during weekends, vacations, and so forth.

 NOTE

The contract might specify that you will respond within 24 hours of a call during weekdays and within 48 hours on weekends and national holidays. This may not seem like an important issue, but it tells the client that you may not respond immediately when they call.

♦ **Equipment.** The contract must specifically state who is to provide the necessary equipment and software for you to perform your support work. This equipment may include PCs, modems, or pagers, depending on the level of support you are expected to provide.

◆ **Type of Support to be Provided.** Specifically state in the contract whether you are to provide just telephone support or whether you are to perform other work as well, such as programming.

◆ **Contract Termination.** Include a clause that lets either you or the client terminate the agreement. Specify how to give the termination notice and how to return equipment.

Business Cards and Keeping in Touch

A big part of the consulting world is networking with other people. Therefore, when leaving a site, make sure that your colleagues can get in touch with you. Have a supply of business cards on hand at least two to three weeks before your last day and hand them out liberally. You will probably collect a few cards as well. When you get a card, write a note on the back that outlines what type of work this person does. After a few years, your memory of who you worked with at prior jobs will fade and you will not remember everyone's name, what they did, or what their strengths were. A goodbye e-mail message to your colleagues is also a good idea.

Keeping in touch with people is difficult. A simple way to keep in touch with key people is to build an e-mail distribution list and to occasionally do mass mailings. Even if the message is just a joke or a Christmas greeting, your name will be kept fresh.

Exit Interviews

Depending on the circumstances of your departure, you may be asked to go through an exit interview. This is especially true if you are the one that initiated the termination of the contract. If for some reason your client has decided to prematurely end your contract, you will want to try to get an exit interview. If you work through to the end of a contract and it is simply not extended, then an exit interview is usually not held.

If you are the one that is leaving the client, during the exit interview your client will probably want to know your reasons for leaving. Put a positive spin on why you are leaving, such as how your new position will offer you more challenges or less traveling. Do not make reference to things such as money if you have not given your client a chance to meet your new offer. Emphasize any positive things that came out of your contract with them, such as new learning experiences. You very well could be looking for a contract with the same client in a few years.

If the client has terminated your contract for some reason, it is good to try to get an exit interview. A lot depends on the reason for the termination, but your main goals during this interview are to find out specifically why you are being terminated. If the reason is not a result of your performance, make sure your client knows that you would be interested in working for them again.

Wrapping Up

When leaving a client site, leave all of your work in a clean and organized fashion. Ideally, the client can find all of your documentation and has the resources in place to take over after you leave. If the client does not have the resources in place to understand what you have done or to do work that you normally would have performed, consider an ongoing service agreement with them. Networking with people is a big part of being a successful SAP consultant.

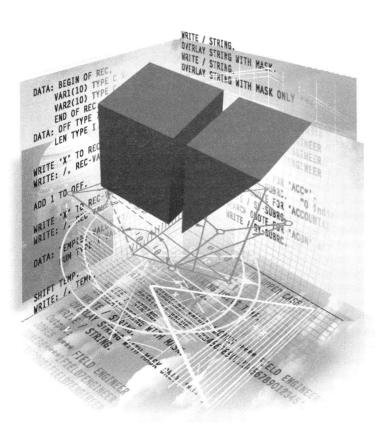

Chapter 11

Workplace Etiquette

To be a good consultant, you need more than just technical knowledge and some experience. Consulting also involves positive interaction with the client and hard work. In the course of a day, good consultants do several things automatically that separate them from the rest of the pack. Some of these workplace mechanics are obvious and simple to do, whereas others require practice and training.

Attitude

Having a positive attitude is a big part of success in the workplace. The key ingredients to success on a new project include the following:

- ◆ **Work hard.** Show dedication to the job and the project. No one can be 100 percent productive for an entire day, but minimize the activities that reduce your output.

- ◆ **Don't complain.** It doesn't matter what you like or don't like; the client is paying you to work. The client doesn't want to hear that you'd rather be doing something else other than working with documentation or test plans; the client just wants it done.

- ◆ **Cooperate.** Throughout our careers, we've been asked to do general typing, update project plans, and help move offices. This may not seem to be a good use of our time, but the client is paying for our services, and if the client wants us to type the occasional letter, we don't hesitate to cooperate.

- ◆ **Be a low maintenance worker.** When bringing on a consultant, a client does not want to deal with personal issues or other things that are not specifically related to the project at hand, including conflicts with other workers, complaints about the speed of the computer, or personal matters.

Drive is a trait of every successful consultant. Successful consultants start earlier, work harder, and stay later. Drive does not just mean working harder; it also means working smarter by being organized and ensuring that you deliver everything that you say you will on time.

When work at a contract slows, many consultants slow with it. A successful consultant looks for more work, starting within the project that the consultant is currently at, and then looks beyond it only if the current client has no work. We have extended several contracts by simply asking for more work when it starts to slow. We are usually given tasks related to the next project the client is thinking of doing. Then, after the current project really does slow, we are natural candidates to continue on to the next project.

Consulting Techniques

Successful employees and consultants have a set of skills that they use in every day business to help them be more productive. Some of these are basic skills that you should know about such as effective listening and writing, others however, may not be so obvious such as effective use of e-mail and meeting management. Some of these skills can come naturally, but all of them can be learned.

Communication

It is very difficult to measure someone's communication effectiveness, but communication is one of a consultant's most important skills. Effective communication can lead to better personal relations with others, which fosters in them a greater sense of trust and confidence in your abilities. In the long run, this can result in more projects being sent in your direction. The most important communication skills for the consultant to develop are effective listening, interacting with others in meetings, and writing.

Effective Listening

An effective listener is able to deliver exactly what the client wants without having to go through many revisions. To be an effective listener:

◆ **Do not interrupt someone or finish their sentences.** Instead, acknowledge your speaker by demonstrating your interest and attention. It is important for the speaker to know that you are paying attention. This can be done either verbally (saying "I see,") or physically (nodding your head and keeping eye contact).

- ◆ **Concentrate on both what the speaker is saying and on the general message that the speaker is conveying.** Eliminate or ignore distractions such as the telephone, passersby, and other noise.

- ◆ **Do not let personal feelings about the speaker effect how you listen.** Focus on the item being discussed.

- ◆ **Pay attention to the content of the message, not its delivery.** When in a conversation, many times people get excited and talk with a lot of emotion, or repeat certain words over and over. Try to ignore this as much as possible and listen to what they are trying to tell you.

- ◆ **Do not form opinions or responses until you have completely understood the message.** Make the conversation a dialog by asking questions as well as by making statements.

- ◆ **Paraphrase the message or idea back to the speaker.** Sometimes you may think you understand what someone has said to you, but if you try to explain it back again, you may find that you do not understand each other at all. This can be a positive reinforcement to the person that you are listening to and understanding what they are saying.

Although listening skills are relatively simple to learn, using them effectively can be difficult. The rewards, however, are numerous and will almost always lead to a better relationship with your client.

Effective Meeting Skills

There are three basic roles that you may play in a meeting: attendee, presenter, or chairperson. Although each role requires different skills, there are some general things that you must do regardless of what role you are playing.

Presenter

If you are making a presentation at a meeting, make sure that all of your materials are in order and that the right equipment is in the room. If you are asked to make a presentation to a client that you have not visited before, it is a good idea to speak with the client before the presentation. During this conversation, you should get an idea of what the client expects you to present and the level of your audience's expertise.

If the purpose of your presentation is to sell a concept or idea, make sure that all of the key people are informed about your idea before the meeting. The purpose of the meeting should be to discuss the components and effects of your idea.

Chairperson

To successfully chair a meeting:

- **Develop an agenda.** This should contain the meeting objective(s), the time the meeting will begin and end, and the preparation expected from each participant.
- **Draw out comments during the meeting.** Turn to people who haven't offered an opinion and ask for one.
- **Deal with people who monopolize the discussion.** You may need to simply interrupt someone and ask for a comment from someone else.
- **Ensure that the meeting does not stray from the intended subject matter.** If the meeting becomes sidetracked, insist that the topic be taken off-line or dealt with during a different meeting.
- **Jot down action items.** Ensure that by the end of the meeting, all the action items are assigned and that there is an agreed-upon date of completion.

Attendee

If you are to attend a meeting, make sure you do the following:

- Before the meeting, find out what preparation work is required and do it.
- During the meeting, actively listen to whomever is speaking and speak only if your points are relevant.
- If you are assigned an action item, ensure that you know its completion date before you leave the meeting as well as who you should contact if you need clarification or more information.

General Meeting Points

Make sure you know each person who will be at a meeting that you are to attend and try to figure out what they want beforehand. For instance, if you are to attend a meeting to decide whether SAP is to replace a legacy system, and you know that one of the other attendees does not think SAP has the same functionality as the legacy system, figure out in advance how to get the functionality that is required in SAP.

Be punctual for meetings; arrive a few minutes early. Every company has its own culture—some are very strict about starting meetings on time, others are not. It doesn't matter which type of company you are working for. Not showing up on time gives the impression of disorganization, not to mention that it also wastes others' time.

Effective Writing Skills

As a writer, you must consider the purpose of your document and analyze your target audience. As you develop your document, you must constantly criticize your work by asking two questions: "Is my document fulfilling its purpose?" and "Is my document presenting the material in a fashion that suits my audience?" When considering your audience, consider what level of detail you need and how the document will be used.

The structure of your document is important. The flow of sections and subsections must be clear and follow a natural course. If possible, get a copy of a similar document done previously for this client. Each client's expectations for a document's format and length varies, and there is no need to waste time making a long document when the client expects a short one.

When writing, follow these general rules:

◆ Always have in mind a specific reader and assume that reader is intelligent but uninformed. It may be useful to state up front what the reader profile is.

◆ Before you begin writing, decide what the report's exact purpose is. Make sure that every sentence makes a contribution to that purpose.

◆ Use language that is simple and familiar.

◆ Make your report attractive to look at, but do not add meaningless frills, such as fonts that arc too fancy.

◆ Always proofread your document before sending it to a client.

Learning Popular Programs

As a highly compensated SAP consultant, most clients won't pay you to learn common software packages to do your job. A consultant that uses the excuse that he doesn't know Microsoft Word, Excel, or Visio gives the impression that he is not up with the latest and greatest, which is exactly what the client is paying for. At a minimum, you should be fairly comfortable using the most popular operating systems, word processors, spreadsheets, project planners, and graphics tools. Become self-reliant with these packages by using the help features. If you go to a client site and do not know how to use one of the popular packages, spend some time outside work hours getting familiar with it. Nearly all clients will understand if a consultant does not know an old or little-known package, but you have no excuse for being unfamiliar with the mainstream programs.

E-mail

Electronic mail is part of nearly every office environment. It is simple to use and can be a very effective communication tool. However, most people do not know how to use it properly. First of all, spell check every e-mail message you send. Though you may not care if someone sends e-mail with a few typos here and there, some people do care. Not only may they interpret this as a rushed message, but they may assume you are a careless person in general. You should read through each message you send out and make sure that it makes sense. People's mailboxes are cluttered enough these days that they will not like having to reread your message several times to understand what you are saying. While you are reading your message, make sure that you are sending this message to only the right people. One final point before sending out a message: remember that messages can be forwarded from one person to another. Be sure that every message you send can pass the Bulletin Board test.

 TIP

The Bulletin Board test

Every message that you send should be able to be posted on a bulletin board and read by everyone. To be safe, never make personal attacks and be sure that you mean everything that you write in each message.

Keep all messages, both those sent and received, no matter how long you have been at a contract. They serve as a good log of your activities and discussions about various aspects of the projects you work on. Nearly all e-mail programs have tools for both searching through messages and for archiving them. If your mailbox has too many messages in it, just archive them off the system or store them on a local drive.

When working on any task, you may have a fairly simple question that a colleague across the aisle or hall could answer quickly. Instead of walking over to the colleague, send the colleague an e-mail message that asks your question. This will prevent interrupting the work of both you and your colleague, and will allow your colleague to answer the question on his or her schedule, which will lead to a well-thought through response. This is not to say that you should never talk to your co-workers. Face to face communication is important, but for many small questions and action items, send an e-mail.

Phone Calls

Personal phone calls should be kept to a strict minimum. Remember that you are working with other employees of the company who may get upset because "the high priced consultant is always on the phone talking to their spouse!" A few idle comments like this, if heard by management, cannot do much good. Also, remember to charge any long distance phone calls that are not specifically related to the work you are doing for a client to your own, or your company's calling card.

One more point about phone calls: If you are meeting with someone in your office and the phone rings, let the voicemail pick it up. Give the person in your office your undivided attention. If there is no voicemail, answer the phone, get the person's name and phone number, and tell them you will call back after your meeting.

Typing Skills

Most people type at the rate of about 20 words per minute, and some consultants still type with just a few fingers. There are several good "typing tutor" programs available, and with a few weeks of practice, 40-50 words per minute is easily obtainable. This may seem like a trivial point, but by being able to type quickly, you accomplish two things.

First, people will be impressed by your typing skills and will receive the impression that you are working efficiently (which you are). Second, you get more work done. Usually consultants spend at least 25 percent of their time just typing documents, e-mail, and so forth. By raising your typing speed from 20 to 40 words per minute, you effectively double your output. If you work an 8-hour day (25 percent of which is typing documents and e-mails), you will have generated 1 more hour of work than the consultants who are still typing at 20 words per minute.

Vacation Time

Everyone needs to take vacation time. If it can be done, it is best to schedule vacations between contracts; however, if you want to take a vacation while working on a contract, make sure that you ask for your client's permission well in advance. Telling a client one or two weeks before you want to go may not leave a good impression. Make sure that you get written approval (e-mail is acceptable) and ensure that you also tell your agency, if you have one. If you are working through an agency, make sure that you follow all of the contractual obligations that exist before asking your client for the vacation time.

Status Reports

Your manager should always know what you are doing. Submitting weekly or monthly status reports is a good method for showing your manager your progress.

Establish a schedule for submitting your report with your manager at the start of the contract and then stick to it. Try to keep the report brief and send it through e-mail if possible. Include these items in your report:

- ◆ Major tasks completed since the last reporting period.
- ◆ Major tasks to be worked on during the next reporting period.
- ◆ Major problems (if any) that you are currently facing and that are preventing you from working effectively. These problems could be related to obtaining information, missing a deadline, waiting for other people to complete tasks that your work is dependent upon, or any other matter that interferes with your work.

Office Politics

Office politics is the art of getting things done. Even those who don't like office politics have to play the game to some degree. If you need to get a client to accept your idea, you require a deliverable from someone, or you need to get two departments to agree on something, then you need to apply office finesse and play office politics. Here are some general rules to follow when playing the game:

- ◆ Never talk negatively about someone else in the company.
- ◆ Follow the chain of command—never bypass a level of management, and when you are going up the chain, make sure that you inform people on the lower rungs that you are doing so.
- ◆ Don't keep secrets from anyone. Communicate everything openly.
- ◆ Don't get in the habit of deal-making. "I'll do this for you if you do this for me" should be avoided.
- ◆ If you make a mistake and offend someone by bypassing the chain of command, talking negatively about him or her, or for some other reason, make a public apology immediately. This does not mean that you need to stand on your desk; an e-mail message will do. Just deal with the situation quickly.

Personal Touch

As mentioned earlier, a successful consultant has a personal touch. It's the little things that count. If you find out the birth date of a co-worker, write it out and remember it. You don't have to do much for the birthday; a card or a balloon is usually enough to show that you remembered and care.

For Christmas, remember your direct supervisor, your agent, your receptionist, and others who play key roles in keeping you employed. When sending presents, consider that many people go on vacation during this time. We usually time presents so that they arrive in the latter part of the second week of December. Flowers, wine, or chocolates make good Christmas presents.

Each person has a different way of keeping track of what they need to do. However you do it, you will end up with some form of an electronic or written list. We walk around with notebooks or hand-held computers that we use for everything—taking notes in meetings, jotting down ideas, and writing To-Do lists. This may not seem glamorous, but it works.

Notebooks give you a chronological list of your work. A large notebook will usually last a few months. Keep them after they are filled. If someone wants to know about a certain material number that had been troublesome three or four weeks ago, it can usually be found in a few minutes by flipping through the notebook.

Work Prioritization

When first starting a contract, work prioritization is usually not that important because you have a very limited number of tasks to perform. As the length of the contract increases and you get to know the client better, your task list will get longer. A good consultant knows how to prioritize tasks to ensure that the important tasks get done on time and that the people who are asking that things get done have the correct expectations.

People respect those who can deliver what they promise when they promised. As a good consultant, you must deliver what you say you will. Proper work prioritization enables you to inform people when you will be able to deliver. Your manager should be involved in the prioritization of work. Managers usually are more in touch with how critical each task is, and involving them in the prioritization process also keeps them involved in your activities.

We often apply the "just-in-time" philosophy. This means that we try to finish tasks just as they are needed and not well in advance. The main reason for this is that the scope of tasks sometimes changes as time goes on. If you finish a task early and the scope changes, you may have to redo your work along with the work of others who are helping you with it. Applying the just-in-time philosophy can be tricky because you must be able to accurately judge how long it will take to complete a certain task. You should also allow for a contingency just in case another task comes along that is more important and is due at the same time.

Make sure that you do not do work just because someone or some department keeps bothering you about it. Make sure that each person understands exactly when you expect to start work on their tasks. If they still bother you about giving higher priority to their tasks, have them convince your manager that their task has a higher priority.

Wrapping Up

Successful consultants are separated from the rest of the pack by their attitude and drive, as well as other habits. You need to exceed the expectations of your colleagues at every opportunity. This involves setting realistic expectations and then working hard to surpass them. Analyze your daily work and interaction with others on a regular basis and find ways to do them better.

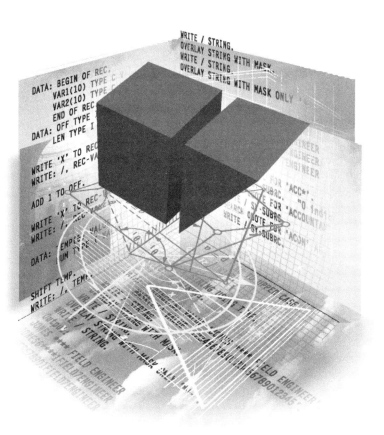

Chapter 12

SAP
Documentation

Documenting your work is probably the most tedious thing you will do. Documentation is a very important part of every consulting job, and it is your professional obligation to provide enough documentation for the client so that the company or another consultant is able to understand what you did and modify and expand your project.

SAP Design Specification

Depending on your role in the SAP implementation (functional, technical, or management), you will either be involved in writing the documentation (functional) or in accepting the initial set of design documents (technical) and following them to create the final solution. Project management is organizing these documents into a meaningful resource for the end user community, so that after the implementation, a library of information is available.

For each solution in an SAP implementation, there must be a design specification. Often, someone will ask you to solve a problem quickly to meet a business need if you are a developer. If you do this without documenting it, then years later someone will face the much larger problem of figuring out what you did and why, before they are able to address a possible upgrade or software replacement. If you are a functional user, by telling your developers to do quick fixes to the system or offer them solutions without pressing for documentation, you leave the implementation incomplete.

Business Requirements

When approaching design documentation, the first specifications that must be written out are the business requirements. In simple terms, "Why are we addressing this issue and what are we hoping to achieve?"

First, determine why your business team is addressing this issue. For example, you may have a process on a legacy system that you wish to replace with a process on SAP, either because the legacy system won't support the new technology or because SAP handles the process better. Whatever the reason, it should be documented for future teams to reference.

Second, address what the solution hopes to achieve. How will this new design provide a solution that satisfies the business users who utilize it? The best way to answer this question is to ask your business user on the design team.

Detail Design

The detail design is where a functional consultant or developer analyzes what implementing this requirement on the system will involve. For example, if a report needs to be written, analyze which preliminary tables in SAP are to be utilized in writing that report. If an interface needs to be written, analyze which transaction needs to be utilized and how often the batch session will be run.

The developer looks at these details and assesses them. The developer determines whether the solution is viable, or whether there is an alternative way to achieve the business requirement.

SAP Support Documentation

When the system has problems, support documentation is necessary for the support staff managing the R/3 system after it is installed.

NOTE

For an in-depth analysis of support documentation, refer to Prima Tech's *Supporting SAP R/3.*

Living Documentation

Living documentation is documentation that incorporates changes (but retains the initial documentation used to build the project) to the project over time. The support documentation should consist of the initial design specifications as well as the detailed design of the project from start to finish. This documentation is very helpful if it is placed where it is accessible to all involved in the SAP implementation.

Because it would require a small warehouse to store all the paperwork containing all the design specifications, it is best to store this documentation on a network drive that is accessible to all necessary personnel and backed up on a regular basis. When a project is modified by adding, deleting, or changing functionality, the person making the modifications can add comments and specifications to the already-existing specifications that are available on the shared network drive. The documentation grows and keeps the project organized, and when an upgrade project for SAP occurs, the business user can do a quick assessment of the code and bolt-ons that were developed in previous years.

SAP Manuals

Some users and SAP professionals attend official SAP training classes. Classes range from technical topics, such as ABAP, to functional classes, such as warehouse management and using the inventory move transaction.

 NOTE

The binders you receive at these functions are great sources of information. In our experience, utilizing the binders in conjunction with online help makes for a great personal documentation library.

Business Procedures

As solutions evolve, business procedures must be written out for new users. From entering new material to configuring the number ranges of the documents managed in the document management system, everything must be documented.

 TIP

A good way to store documentation is to keep it on a networked drive where everyone has access. This way you do not have to maintain a library of binders for every solution.

Referencing Online Documentation

SAP has some great online documentation. Using the graphical user interface, navigate from HELP to EXTENDED HELP and type in any topic. SAP will provide whatever documentation is available via this method, assuming that your BASIS (SAP Administration) team installed the online documentation correctly.

SAP In-Line Code Documentation

Documentation is extremely important if you change actual SAP code. First, you should be a fairly experienced consultant before you start changing SAP code. You should understand the implications of your changes, both technically and in the resulting business process. Documentation is important because in the future your client will upgrade its SAP system whether the client likes it or not. During this upgrade process, undocumented custom changes to SAP code will disappear as the new upgraded system is copied over the existing system. If the changes are documented, both in the code as well as in documentation that the client has access to, then the upgraded SAP can be copied into the system, even though it will overwrite the customized code. After installing the SAP upgrade, a business analysis can be done to determine whether the custom change needs to be reapplied (perhaps the upgrade took care of the need for the change). If it is still needed, then it can be reapplied using the information in the documentation.

The first set of modifications to SAP code might be provided as OSS (Online Service System) notes. OSS notes are fixes and upgrades provided to SAP customers to fix known bugs and provide more functionality to certain releases of SAP. SAP provides a printable sheet from the R/3 system (see Listing 12-1).

Listing 12-1

```
Number 0040217
Version 0003 from 12.12.1996
Status Released for customer
Set by SAP AG on 12.12.1996

Language E
Short text EDI invoice receipt: Error in the syntax check
```

Administrator SAP AG

Component BC-ABC-SC System components, screen, Batch Input

Long text

Symptom

During the syntax check in the function group 'IEDI' (program SAPLIEDI), you get the message

'Field "C_WF_RESULT_OK" is unknown. It is neither contained in one of the entered tables not defined by a "DATA" statement

EDI invoice receipt, however, still runs without a syntax error.

Additional key words

INVOIC

Cause and preconditions

Program error.

Solution

Corrected in Release 3.0E. Advance corrections: Install the following correction.

Source code corrections

Program SAPLIEDI:

```
********************************************************************
* System-defined Include-files. *
********************************************************************
INCLUDE LIEDITOP .
*NCLUDE MBDCONWF. "DELETE
INCLUDE LIEDIUXX.
...


Program LIEDITOP:


...
*_____.*
* COMMON DATA *
*_____.*
```

```
INCLUDE FM06EC08.
INCLUDE MBDCONWF. "INSERT
```

```
Valid releases
```

```
R/3 standard 300 - 30D
```

```
Further components
```

```
BC-ABA-SC System components, screen, Batch Input
MM-IV Invoice Verification
Page 2
```

OSS notes tell you how to reconfigure certain SAP settings and offer strategies to make your R/3 system more efficient. For this particular OSS note, comment out the old code and insert the new code. Insert comments on the side of the commented code as well as the new code with the OSS number next to it. At the top of the code change implemented by OSS, enter an asterisk with your initials or name, the date, and the OSS note number you are applying. At the end of the OSS change, insert another commented line that marks the end of changes.

While some changes to the R/3 system are made at the request of SAP and are documented by the OSS system, other changes will be made to your system by customer request. This does not mean that you must not note the changes. These other types of modifications made to SAP source code are motivated by a customer request. Obviously, the first task is to determine whether SAP has already provided a fix that addresses this customer request in its OSS system. Search the OSS system, and if you don't find an SAP-provided fix to the client's request, then address the change on your own. Once you have found a solution to the client's request, implement it in the code, just as you would implement an OSS note. The only difference is that instead of an OSS note number, insert the customer request number, which refers back to the well-documented design specifications that justify the request (see Listing 12-2).

Listing 12-2

```
*Modification #3
*GMD 12/01/98
SELECT SINGLE * FROM MARC WHERE "MOD 3
MATNR = W_MATNR AND "MOD 3
WERKS = W_WERKS. "MOD 3
*SELECT * FROM MARC WHERE "MOD 3
* MATNR = W_MATNR. "MOD 3
WRITE:/ MARC-MATNR,
20 MARC-WERKS.
*ENDSELECT. "MOD 3
*End Modification #3
```

New Code Development

Any new code development should start out with a documentation template. Listing 12-3 contains a template that you can use to develop your program. You can download this template from Prima Tech's Web site for this book at **www.prima-tech.com**

Listing 12-3

```
REPORT ZTEMPLATE.
*_____*
* Date:
* Author:
* Description:
*
*_____*
* Change Description:
* Change Author:
* Change Date:
*
*
*_____*
*
*_____Table Declaration_____*
```

```
*-------------Internal Table Declaration----------*


*-------------Data Declaration-----------------*

*-------------Selection Screen----------------*

*-------------Start of Selection Event---------*
START-OF-SELECTION.



*-------------End of Selection Event-----------*
END-OF-SELECTION.



*-------------Begin of Main Program-------------.*



*-------------Other Events--------------------*
AT SELECTION-SCREEN.

*-------------Begin of Forms-----------------*
```

While new development is documented, there is also room for documentation for future changes. Once the documentation is present in the code, the next person who modifies the code will update the documentation.

Modification of Existing Programs

Sometimes you will need to make modifications to existing programs. Make sure to document these programs as you would a new program. This does not mean you need to go back and make sure you understand and document the entire source code if you are only adding one line, but use the ZTEMPLATE program as the basis of your new code and keep a log of changes at the header of the program. Place code comments inside the code where you have made the changes.

At the header of the program, type in code changes, the purpose of the changes, and tie the code changes to the design document. Inside the actual code, insert comments that refer to the header documentation, which shows what the changes are (see Listing 12-4).

Listing 12-4

```
*Modification #3
*GMD 12/01/98
SELECT SINGLE * FROM MARC WHERE "MOD 3
MATNR = W_MATNR AND "MOD 3
WERKS = W_WERKS. "MOD 3
*SELECT * FROM MARC WHERE "MOD 3
* MATNR = W_MATNR. "MOD 3
WRITE:/ MARC-MATNR,
20 MARC-WERKS.
*ENDSELECT. "MOD 3
*End Modification #3
```

Generally, we comment out the old code that we are modifying or deleting, even if we need to type it back into the program. That way, if someone wants to cancel our change, they just need to uncomment the old code and comment our code, and the correction is made.

Wrapping Up

As an SAP professional, you will be at a project for at least one week and possibly for years on end. It is imperative that you document your procedures, solutions, and code to ensure that the person who inherits your responsibilities has enough information to do their job. Documentation is not the most exciting job in the world, but it is part of being a good SAP consultant.

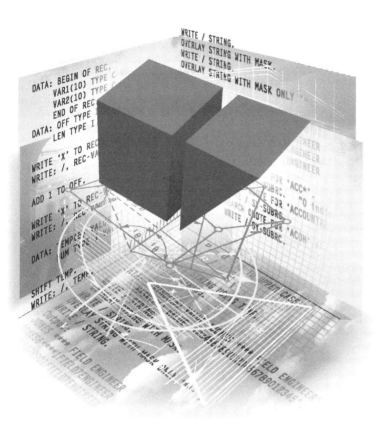

Chapter 13

Certification

SAP certification is generally a mysterious realm for new SAP professionals. SAP has begun to establish itself in the Fortune 500 marketplace, but it still needs to obtain a higher level of respect in this area. In the past, SAP knowledge has been enough to give you an edge on the other guy. However, in today's market, to give you that extra edge, consider becoming certified.

The Importance of Certification

Why become SAP certified? While there is currently a shortage of SAP talent in the marketplace, the required courses can be very expensive and even difficult to enroll in. Though some veteran SAP consultants may be be able to test out of such classes, there remain several sensible reasons to obtain certification. Your first and foremost purpose as a consultant is to make your client comfortable with your level of skill and confident that you have the expertise to carry out the work they require. Certification ensures an employer that you know SAP according to SAP's high standards.

Also, as SAP becomes more widely recognized and new people get into the R/3 market, competition will become more and more intense. Having certification on your résumé makes you look more professional and more respectable to your clients and colleagues. An SAP manager wants to feel comfortable that the company's multimillion-dollar R/3 system is being entrusted to someone who can do the job. Certification ensures that you have reached a certain level of R/3 competence.

A Client's Preference

The one thing that SAP lacks is a large number of qualified and competent people to install and customize the R/3 systems. Consequently, many applicants may submit more "creative" résumés about their experience. Additionally, references of consultants from overseas are harder to confirm. So, with quite a few clients having been burned in the past by consultants claiming to be more qualified than they actually are, background and reference checks have become commonplace in the R/3 consulting market.

Although most clients do not insist that their consultants be certified by SAP, the trend is moving in that direction. A client that prefers certified consultants is simply insisting that the minimum ability level of a consulting team is sufficient to pass the SAP certification tests. While this practice does not guarantee that the consulting team is an excellent one, it will probably become steadily more widespread among employers over the next few years.

A More Formal Education

Another trend in the SAP world is the change in the SAP AG company itself. SAP has started to expand and change how it does business. Clients in the past have complained about the quality of the training classes from SAP. As a result of this, SAP AG has improved the program and increased the scope of the partner academy. SAP will probably begin to recommend to its clients that all the consultants that they hire should be SAP certified, just as Microsoft recommends NT-certified professionals and Oracle recommends Oracle-certified database administrators.

The Big Six

Another reason to seek certification is so that you can remain competitive among consultants from large consulting firms, notably the Big Six. While the Big Six has actually become the Big Three in the last year, the term *Big Six* is still applied to the large consulting and accounting firms. Large consulting firms require strong credentials, so if a large consulting firm is heading up the project you will be working on, your résumé should reflect excellence. Certification will give you an edge over a comparable consultant sitting next to you in the lobby, waiting for an interview.

Experience Path

There are two paths to certification. If you are an experienced SAP consultant, it is possible to forego the lengthy classes and just take the test. The other path is to take the required classes at the SAP Partner Academy and then pass the examination. The classes generally take four weeks (see Figure 13-1).

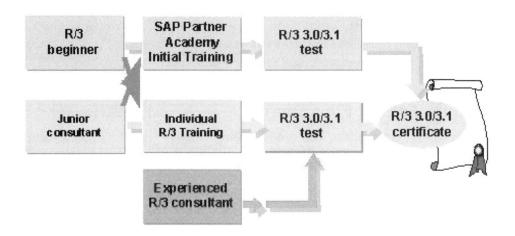

FIGURE 13-1 *The paths to SAP certification*

The Letters

Besides having two years of experience, you must have a letter confirming that you have demonstrated proficiency in the area you wish to be certified in. This letter must be signed by an SAP alliance manager. Generally, each client has an alliance manager. A good strategy is to develop a friendship with that manager so that you can write the letter and have them sign it.

You must then contact the SAP Partner Academy in your area and fax them the letter. Then pick a test date and make your plane reservations, and budget for a little time to study.

The Tests

The examination covers specific product releases of the R/3 system as well as business processes, effective implementation practices, and technical know-how. Generally, the tests are given along with SAP Partner Academy courses. However, consultants with sufficient SAP experience can take the test to become certified without taking the courses.

SAP does not provide study guides for the tests. The best way to find out about the test and its contents is to study the SAP online help CD and talk with friends who are already certified. Books will be available soon in regard to what to study for the certification.

The test is three hours for each topic, and there are 180 multiple choice questions. You have access to an R/3 system throughout the test.

Certification Process

The formalized certification process is through the partner academy. First, the individual takes a class, and then takes a test at the end of each class. If the individual passes the test, then they are granted certification.

The Classes

At the academy, five application tracks (see Table 13-1), two technical tracks (see Table 13-2), and four advanced studies are offered (see Table 13-3).

Table 13-1 Application Tracks at the SAP Partner Academy

Subject	Abbreviation
Financials/Controlling	(FI)
Production Planning	(PP)
Materials Management	(MM)
Sales and Distribution	(SD)
Human Resources	(HR)

Table 13-2 Technical Tracks at the SAP Partner Academy

Subject
Technical Consultant Training
ABAP Development Workbench

Table 13-3 Advanced Studies at the SAP Partner Academy

Subject
SAP Business Workflow Products
Application Link Enabling (ALE)
SAP R/3 Business Engineering Workbench (BEW)
Internet Capabilities

The Test

The test is just like the test administered to the advanced consultant who bypasses the class. The test consists of 180 multiple choice questions based on the material presented in the class, and is administered online for three hours. During the exam, you have access to SAP online help.

Wrapping Up

SAP certification is a great option for the SAP R/3 consultant for two reasons. First, the course material will enhance your knowledge of SAP. Second, if you already have this information under your belt, SAP certification gives you the seal of approval from SAP AG. This seal of approval enhances your credibility in the eyes of your clients and in the eyes of your business colleagues.

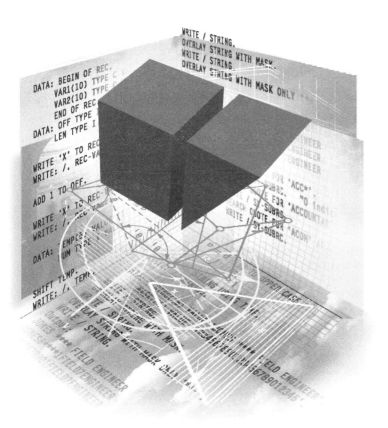

Chapter 14

Training

Whether through SAP courses, third-party training, or hands-on experience, it is essential that you keep your skills sharp. While getting into SAP courses can be a challenge, there are several strategies that can help you do this. Why train? You are only as valuable as what your skills are. Forget what you are being paid or who you know; if your skills are not current, you will become extinct as an SAP professional.

SAP Courses

SAP AG offers a comprehensive training regimen for its partners and its client's employees. Currently, SAP offers training in certain areas, or *focuses*. There are two avenues of technical classes in the BASIS area.

The ABAP (Advanced Business Application Programming) developer begins with a course in ABAP, Screen, and Menu Painter, and a system administrator begins with a system architecture class and moves on to Security Objects and database administration in relation to SAP R/3.

Besides the technical track, there are module-specific areas that range from general business knowledge to configuring a system. These classes are divided into modules, and then into business and configuration classes. There are also general user classes on how to use the system. Sending an advanced user to take this course and then to train their team back at the company's site is beneficial.

A current catalog of SAP courses can be found on the SAP Web site. If you navigate to **www.sap.com** and then click the Services, Education Service links, the current SAP class offerings page will be displayed (**www.sap.com/service/traiserv.htm**).

 NOTE

An excellent resource is Prima Tech's *What Every Business Needs to Know about SAP*. It discusses education requirements for each member on the installation team.

These classes are divided into version-specific courses, delta courses, and partner academy courses. Version-specific courses discuss the topics as they relate to a certain version of SAP. Delta courses are designed to take your training from one version of SAP to the next version. The partner academy offers in-depth classes that are designed to produce certified SAP consultants. The partner academy generally trains in the current release of SAP.

If you have access to an R/3 system, the current classes available along with the number of slots left in each class is available through the OSS system. Your OSS administrator should have instructions on how to obtain this information.

Requesting a Catalog

In the United States, SAP can be reached at the telephone numbers listed in Table 14-1. Other SAP office contact numbers can be found at the SAP Web page (**www.sap.com**). Click Contact Us to find the office nearest you.

Table 14-1 SAP Office Contact Numbers

City	Phone Number
Atlanta	(404) 943-2900
Austin	(512) 425-2300
Boston	(617) 672-6500
Chicago	(708) 947-3400
Cincinnati	(513) 977-5400
Cleveland	(216) 615-3000
Dallas	(972) 868-2000
Denver	(303) 740-6696
Detroit	(248) 304-1000
Houston	(713) 917-5200
Miami	(305) 476-4400
Minneapolis	(612) 359-5000
New York	(212) 346-5300
Philadelphia	(610) 595-4900
Pittsburgh	(412) 255-3795

Table 14-1 SAP Office Contact Numbers *(continued)*

City	Phone Number
San Francisco	(415) 637-1655
Seattle	(206) 462-6395
St. Louis	(314) 213-7500

When speaking with SAP, ask for a catalog and to be put in touch with their education center. SAP prefers to send these catalogs to partners and clients, so if you can have a catalog sent to your client, your chance of receiving it increases significantly.

Third-Party Courses

Over the last year, third-party companies began offering training courses. One such training company is Coresoft Corporation, which has offices in California, Georgia, and Virginia. Coresoft currently offers courses in business application areas such as financial and materials management, and in technical areas such as ABAP and EDI.

You will need to determine whether a third-party vendor such as Coresoft can provide the training that you need. The advantage to attending courses at a company such as Coresoft is that the classes are not limited to partners and customers of SAP. Any person can pay money and take these courses. However, SAP courses remain the most appealing on a résumé, so look for official SAP training courses first, if at all possible

 NOTE

Coresoft can be reached for a catalog at (800) 879-6458 or on the Web at **www.coresoftcorp.com**.

Sponsorship

To take SAP courses on your own through SAP is impossible. An SAP client or partner must sponsor you, even if you are paying your own way. However, as an independent consultant, it is often to your client's benefit that you attend these classes. If this is the case, perhaps you can get your client to sponsor you and pay for the class. If not, maybe the client will just sponsor you (more realistic) and have your consulting company pay. At worst, you will have to pay for the course.

Your client's sponsorship to attend SAP AG's classes depends mainly on the rapport that you have developed with them. If the client feels very comfortable with you as a consultant, then your chances of going to SAP under the client's banner increase significantly.

If the client elects to pay, find out the date and location, call SAP to reserve a spot, and attend. If you or your consulting company need to pay for it, reimburse your client for the expense of the class, because SAP will only accept purchase orders from its clients and partners.

Wrapping Up

SAP certification and formal training will not guarantee your SAP consulting success. However, combined with hard work and good old fashioned experience, these two positives make a powerful combination on any successful SAP consultant's resume.

For the new consultant, and for delta implementations, SAP courses are very valuable. The courses can be taken through SAP directly, if you have an affiliation with a partner or client of SAP, or through private companies. These private companies are third-party vendors that charge for the courses, and consulting firms that have internal training programs. Depending on the state (USA) in which you sign your employment contract, you may be obligated legally for the duration of your contract in exchange for these classes and SAP experience. The courses make your résumé, as well as your presence with the client, appear more credible. Hands-on experience can only be found on the job, but technical knowledge can be found in the classes or in the *SAP Series* books by Prima Tech (**www.prima-tech.com**).

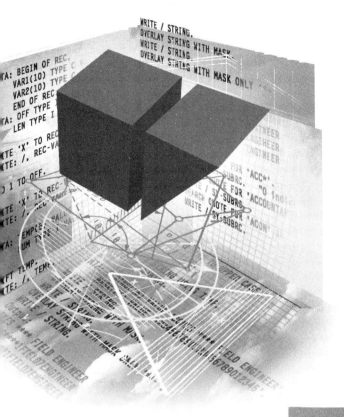

PART III

SAP Architecture

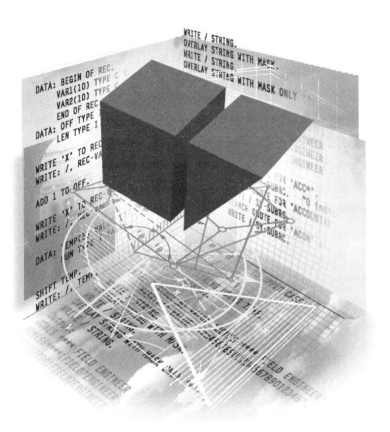

Chapter 15

New
Implementations

New implementations of SAP are very challenging for the SAP professional. The main focus of the work is to make the transition from the existing legacy system(s) to SAP as painless as possible for the client while setting up a solid foundation for supporting the system in the future. This must be accomplished while making sure that all existing legacy system functionality is still incorporated in the new SAP system. In the following pages, you'll learn how to interface with legacy system programmers, mentor to people new to SAP, and spot potential pitfalls on a new project.

Starting on the Right Foot

The key to all successful implementations is starting the project correctly. The first few weeks of a project will define the expectations and methodology that will be used for the lifetime of the project, and are critical for a well-run project. We have been on new implementations that were not well-defined in the beginning, and these projects took nearly twice as long to implement.

If you are on a project during its first few weeks, part of your role is to ensure that no major mistakes are made. This does not mean that you need to run the project, but instead monitor how the project manager is setting things up. If you notice something that does not seem right or an area that needs more work, it is your responsibility to point this out and offer solutions. Some things to watch out for during the first few weeks are the following:

- ◆ Keep everything as simple as possible
- ◆ Ensure that the business reengineering methodology is defined
- ◆ Ensure that the client has a good strategy for modifying SAP
- ◆ Ensure that standards are defined for all aspects of the project
- ◆ Review staffing requirements at the various stages of the project
- ◆ Examine the infrastructure and determine what should be in place for a successful project

Keeping It Simple

Many projects start with a grand scheme of replacing all the legacy systems with SAP at once. This is usually doomed to fail because the task of coordinating the financial, materials management, procurement, sales, human resources, and other areas simultaneously is monumental in a large organization.

The key to successfully implementing SAP is to keep everything as simple as possible. This usually means doing a phased-in implementation, which allows the company to focus on a few business areas at a time and allows each area to stabilize before implementing the next set of modules.

The Big Bang method poses several potential hazards for the company installing SAP. The first is that the implementation does not properly implement or takes a long time to stabilize. This disrupts the normal business flow and can mean large cash losses for the company. Another potential problem is having a whole set of new users working on all the SAP modules at once. This requires extra staffing for a fairly significant amount of time because the new users need extra training in the new SAP environment.

The phased-in implementation does have its own set of complications because additional interfaces need to be written to communicate with legacy systems that have not been converted. Another potential problem with the phased-in implementation method is that oversights in earlier implementations may be discovered when working on the later stages. This can usually be avoided by having experienced people working on how the entire SAP implementation will be phased in at the beginning of the project.

Which modules to start with depends entirely on the business, but the finance module is typically the first to go in. This is because the finance side of nearly all businesses is run roughly the same, and most legacy systems have existing interfaces to the finance systems that can be modified easily to integrate with SAP.

Historical Data

Historical data includes closed purchase orders (PO), old product data changes, and old quotations. A client can retrieve this data from the legacy system after SAP has gone live. Converting historical data is a time-consuming task because it involves setting up a whole set of new interfaces and dummy transactions.

CAUTION

Do not import historical data into SAP unless a specific business area requires that historical data be converted and imported. If it hasn't already been done, the technical members of the implementation team need to receive concentrated ABAP/4 training. This training ensures that they can effectively write data manipulation programs, interfaces, and reports within SAP. For more information on training, please refer to Chapter 14.

Consider, for example, the conversion of closed POs. To get the closed purchase orders into the SAP system, you must create the purchase orders, receive the goods, pay the invoices, and so forth. To do all of this and keep the current inventory levels, vendor information, and financial accounts correct requires a fair bit of work. Historical data can be used by various areas to determine marketing and production trends. If this is a major goal of your client, then install a system such as SAP's Business Information Warehouse (BW) and store the historical data there.

Converting from a Legacy System

When data has to be converted from a legacy system, the easiest and the cheapest way is to first format it for SAP programs. SAP has programs for importing many kinds of data, and you can usually modify these programs to fit your specific needs. Legacy programmers are already familiar with their application data, the systems they reside on, and the company-specific terminology, so they should be able to write extract programs to meet SAP input file criteria. Sometimes this involves a bit of work on the SAP side to write small programs to push data to the legacy side (i.e., old/new material number cross-references or the contents of critical check-tables).

Reengineering

Most organizations take the opportunity to do some business reengineering when they install SAP. Our philosophy is to keep the business reengineering limited to eliminating nonstandard business practices and current unsound solutions so that the new implementation conforms to what a standard SAP system can be configured to do. Doing too much reengineering while installing SAP can make the whole project very complicated and can lead to numerous delays as the various business areas attempt to agree on how the business should operate.

There is also the issue of business continuity. Installing SAP is usually a fairly large shock to a business to begin with, and adding new business processes along with the SAP installation can be disruptive to a company's business flow.

Modification of SAP

When a client decides to adopt the SAP system, they usually have several legacy systems to replace. The client is probably used to the idea of being able to modify these legacy systems to meet whatever needs they have and may expect to be able to do the same with SAP. Modifications to SAP should be highly discouraged from the beginning of the project. By modifications, we mean direct modifications to core SAP source code, screens, customizations, and tables where SAP has not provided a way to make the change. It is okay to write reports or to add additional functionality, and SAP even encourages this by providing many user exits throughout the programs. SAP has been installed by thousands of companies over a very broad range of industries.

If a client mentions that their business is different and that standard SAP will not work, they should probably consider reengineering to streamline their operations. This is not always possible or practical for a company, but it should be a trigger for you. At a minimum, you should identify why the client cannot function within SAP boundaries and make sure that the reason is valid.

Standards

All well-run projects have a clearly-defined set of standards from the start of the project, and stick with them for the life of the project. These standards encompass customizations, coding, documentation, decision-making procedures, and issue resolution. Time should be spent at the beginning of a project to figure out the proper channels to go through to get things done. A clear definition of a single person or position that will take responsibility for each and every area within the project is crucial. When there are disputes over a specific area, a clearly outlined procedure on the resolution will speed the decision-making process and make the whole project run smoother.

Standards should be adopted for defining business requirements, coding, documentation for both code and customizations, application of OSS (Online Service System) notes, office software packages to be used, and storage of documents.

OSS Notes

Consider, for example, the application of OSS notes. If no standards are established at the start of the project, you have several people installing the notes with no central log of what was applied or to which environment each note was transported. This can lead to a lot of extra work later as some people try to reapply notes or determine which notes need to be transported to a production system.

On a new project, you should be aware of any area that seems to lack a uniform approach and bring this to management's attention. Ideally, you will also propose what the standard should be or at least who should be involved in the development of the procedure.

Staffing

Many projects incur cost overruns simply because they do not have appropriate staffing at each phase of the project. Part of an SAP professional's job is to ensure that the client is made aware of the staffing required, particularly at the beginning of the project. Sometimes, many people from a company start taking SAP courses haphazardly for the various business and technical areas, and then try to figure out how to install SAP with this newfound knowledge. This inevitably leads to cost overruns because these individuals do not have SAP experience. This can happen even with installations that are managed by outside consulting firms if good controls are not put in place from the beginning.

At the beginning, it is crucial to have a limited number of people defining the project's overall scope. This core team should consist of the following people (the number of people depends on the scope of the project, but usually one or two from each area is enough):

- Personnel from the client who have an excellent comprehension of the business side of the company
- Technical persons from the legacy environment who understand how the current legacy systems work and how they interact with each other
- SAP business analysts

◆ Technical SAP analysts

◆ Project manager

This small team should be able to fulfill all the necessary duties of the planning stages of implementing SAP. The members of this team should all be highly qualified in their fields. These team members will not come cheaply, but this cost will pay for itself many times over during the lifetime of the project.

Once the core team is established, the general game plan for implementing SAP can be determined in fairly broad terms. After this stage, more people can be brought on to do the actual work of SAP functional setup, business reengineering, programming, testing, etc.

Programmers and functional specialists are also necessary to the project, at a price. Functional specialists are the people who guide the initial transition between the legacy and SAP systems. These specialists determine how the SAP system is to be configured to meet the needs of the client in each functional area. They learn about the current legacy environment and then configure SAP to operate in a similar manner. Mistakes made at this point are costly, as many other people will be making decisions based on these initial settings.

Experienced ABAP (Advanced Business Application Programming) programmers can code a new solution better and faster than a team of people with little experience. Even small programs such as reports can cost a lot of money if they do not perform properly or are not coded correctly. Once the programming is done, most of the experienced programmers can be let go. Many projects keep their programming staff around too long, as all that's usually necessary at the end of a project is a few experienced people to catch the last-minute bugs and to write last-minute reports.

When a fully functional prototype system becomes available, it is time to start training some of the client's staff who will be using the system. Start with a small group and work out any kinks in the training before the training begins en masse. The people involved in the system's testing can become the superusers and can be used to help train the other people.

Infrastructure

The general infrastructure also needs to be defined early in a project, including hardware requirements, networks, client definitions for the various SAP environments, and code and customization movement between the various systems.

As a consultant on a new project, you must ensure that you understand how the various parts of this infrastructure function and alert management if you notice any problems.

Legacy Systems

A new SAP installation replaces one or more legacy systems. These legacy systems contain data that may need to be brought over to SAP. The legacy programs and data contain all of the exceptions to the standard business model that the design of the new SAP implementation must handle. The keepers of this knowledge are the existing legacy support and program staff, some of whom may be on the SAP implementation team. Keeping these people in touch with current developments in the SAP project is a good idea, as they will be able to point out possible design flaws in the new SAP solution. Include these people in the design and configuration of the SAP system.

New Development

New development on any SAP project is challenging. It is even more so on new installations of SAP because there are usually a number of areas co-developing at the same time, and there is no opportunity to do integration testing until everyone has finished. There are also the inevitable design changes based on changes required in other areas that are first discovered during their unit test phase. For this reason, it is best to delay new development in each area as long as possible and to let other areas that require longer lead times start first.

 NOTE

If there is a design change in your area, make sure that you communicate this to all other areas that may be affected. This is not just for their benefit; other areas may find problems in your design changes that you did not see.

New development is also more difficult on new projects because there is no methodology in place for procedures such as data archiving and security profiles. These have to be defined and implemented. For details on various aspects of new development, refer to Chapter 18, "Design."

Client Involvement

Getting all areas involved in the implementation at the right time is important both in designing the solution and getting it approved. If some areas are left out or do not buy into the design, the time and expense involved in implementing increases dramatically.

Depending on the type of consulting you do, you may not have much control over this area. You can, however, still do things to help. Ensure that you have an open communication channel to each business and technical area that you have to deal with and keep them informed of the progress and problems that you are having. You can gain acceptance from different areas by trying to get them to suggest solutions to your problems instead of just criticizing your solution.

Establishing a Release Version

A challenge in a new SAP installation is determining which version of SAP will be targeted for the production environment. SAP is constantly upgrading and improving its product and is always only a few months away from the next release. The easiest and best approach is to take the current stable release version and stick with it throughout the project. Changing major releases of SAP during the middle of the project is very disruptive; even a minor release upgrade can cause problems, as you will have to examine all the areas that are already done to see if they are affected by the upgrade.

New SAP Functionality

It is difficult to set up a timeline for a new implementation that is dependent on new SAP functionality that does not yet exist or is in its infancy (e.g., ATP servers or Internet Transaction Server). Ensure that your client has contingency plans to handle delays in the release of the functionality.

Also ensure that your client understands that going with leading edge software from SAP has a definite cost associated with it. When SAP ships brand-new functionality, there are usually some initial flaws in it that will take time to find and fix. There is likely to be some missing functionality that will either have to be coded by the client or worked around. Most of the time spent coding or working around the missing functionality will be at your client's expense, and the client should be made aware of this.

OSS Note Applications

If the client is on an early release of a new version of SAP (e.g., 4.5a) it is very important to scan through SAP's Online Service System (OSS) regularly. Though SAP can supply hot patches for critical bugs, many notes are not included and should be researched to see if they apply to your installation.

TIP

Regardless whether you are a technical or functional professional, make sure that OSS is checked for your area.

Training

At the beginning of a new implementation, there is usually a high number of employees with low levels of experience in SAP. It is part of your job to mentor these people and to provide them with more efficient ways to do things. The type of mentoring needed varies and depends on your line of consulting. The following sections outline some of the general areas of SAP and the things you should be on the lookout for in each.

Infrastructure Personnel

Infrastructure tasks include monitoring the Unix systems, dealing with transports, reorganizing tables, maintaining SAP logins, and other day-to-day things that need to be done just to keep the SAP system running. Taking care of the infrastructure of an SAP system is not much different than taking care of other legacy environment systems.

The main area usually overlooked within the general training scheme for infrastructure personnel is the knowledge of basic SAP programming skills. Learning how SAP works from a technical point of view is much easier if there is also a basic understanding of ABAP and the data dictionary. Such understanding helps clarify how things such as code transports, authorization objects, OSS notes, enqueue locks, and indexes on tables are used with SAP, and how they relate to the day-to-day tasks that an infrastructure team performs.

Business Analysts

There is a tendency for people to try to adapt SAP to mimic their old legacy environment. Your job as a consultant is to work with these individuals and get them thinking in SAP terms. Showing business analysts new to SAP the various reports that come with the SAP system and how the reports integrate will help them adjust and benefit from the new features. It is also useful to examine the old legacy system to see what type of functionality and reporting it provides and then to show people how you can get the same information (in a different format) from SAP.

A common complaint from business analysts new to SAP is that SAP is harder to use than their legacy systems. This is usually because legacy systems are not as strict as SAP in the area of data integrity. Explain to the business analysts that this integrity will result in an overall smoother system with fewer problems later on (their legacy system must have some problems, otherwise why would they be converting over to SAP?). Being able to communicate effectively with the business analysts is another good reason to become familiar with the old legacy system.

Programmers

New SAP programmers need mentoring because of the high level of integration within SAP and the lack of documentation on how the system is put together. The two areas in which experienced programmers who are new to SAP make the most mistakes are incorrect or inefficient use of SAP functionality and the improper selection of data.

The only way that the incorrect or inefficient use of SAP functionality can be corrected is for all code to go through a code review process by an experienced ABAP programmer. The reviewer checks to see that programs are both correct and efficient. The review should not be treated as a test, but as a learning experience for the novice programmer.

Although the improper selection of data should be picked up during the code review, sometimes it is missed. Also, programs that run against data on the development or consolidation system sometimes have different kinds of data than that on the production version, which results in different response times. At any rate, if improperly selected data are missed during the code review, these problems can be picked up by examining short dumps (for online reports that time out) or through examining the system performance through transactions like SM66. You should also arrange to conduct or organize a refresher ABAP course for novice programmers after they have three to six months of SAP programming experience. At this stage, they should have enough experience to comprehend a lot more of the course information than when they first took the course.

End Users

There is a tendency in new installations to train end users too early. Training should be provided at the last possible moment and a refresher course should be provided about one month after the system has gone live.

Having superusers around also helps in the training of end users. Most people do not catch on to simple things such as program variants and searching via matchcodes during the training classes. After working for a while with SAP, it will be easier for them to learn these simple things, as they will not be trying to understand the basics of SAP.

Testing

Testing the SAP solution prior to going live is probably the second most critical part of the SAP implementation process (the first month of the project is the most critical). This means testing the whole system with all of the various modules working together. Thorough integration testing will uncover any flaws in design or errors that have been made, and it's much cheaper to find these errors before the system goes live rather than fix them up afterward. As an SAP professional on a new project, insist that your area is thoroughly tested with all areas that it may integrate with.

You should also ensure that the data you are testing against accurately depicts what the production environment will look like. Any report will run quickly against a small database, but tables (such as BSEG and MSEG) can become huge in a production environment, and the same reports may not work there.

Dry Runs

Dry runs are the practice runs prior to the actual go-live event. Usually the dry runs include the last synchronization of transactional data from old legacy systems and transportation of the last code/data objects to the production environment. As a consultant at this stage of the SAP installation, you will want to ensure that there is a project plan set up with each step outlined. Remember to include items such as dependencies on other steps and personnel contacts when each step is done. Microsoft Project is an inexpensive and practical tool for this task.

One of the goals at this stage is to get some idea of the time it will take to get the production system up. If you set up the build plan in Microsoft Project, you can assign actual duration times to each item and then have it calculate the total time (including intertask dependencies).

 CAUTION

One thing that is often overlooked during dry runs is the testing of Security profiles. This can be a big problem the first day a system goes live. Make sure you test them during the dry run.

If your build plan is fairly large (24 hours or longer), you will want to ensure that your client has scheduled database backups in the plan. A system failure or a data load program used incorrectly at a late stage of a build can cause big delays to the starting of the SAP system. These delays can translate into a big financial loss for your client.

Going Live

Nothing quite prepares you for the initial starting of the new production system of SAP (typically named *Go-Live*). During this hectic time there is usually a large area of the company that has never used the SAP system and is suddenly online. Depending on the type of installation, you may be asked to work very long hours or be on-call, 24 hours per day, 7 days per week, during the initial phase of the SAP startup.

You will probably be one of the few people on-site with major SAP experience, and your client will be counting on you for leadership in dealing with problems, training, and other issues. You must make sure that people, especially the ones new to SAP and system startups, take the production environment very seriously.

There should be no code rushed into production simply because something is wrong. All code must be reviewed. Often people get excited during the go-live event and are willing to skip this basic step. SAP is much-less forgiving than many legacy systems when it comes to incorrect data because it is so tightly integrated.

NOTE

Consider, for example, a case where someone loads the material master records with the wrong average price. You cannot just reload these records after the system has gone live. You must make sure that this average price was not used in any price determination for purchase orders and that they were not stored in any SAP Information System records.

Don't plan for vacations directly before, during, or immediately after a go-live event. This shows a lack of responsibility or a lack of commitment to getting the job done on your part.

If you don't have a pager or cell phone, insist that the client provide you with one so that you are reachable 24 hours per day for the initial month or so of the new SAP system.

Stabilization Period

The stabilization period is the time between going-live and the cessation of daily crises; in other words, it is when all of the major interfaces, reports, and processes are working smoothly. Closely monitor during the stabilization matters such as problems with the job schedules and backups, and growth in database tables.

During the stabilization period, try to get a feel for how much longer your contract will last, unless it is a fixed-length contract. If you like working for the client, you may want to start inquiring about SAP installations in other areas within the same company, or see if they are interested in keeping you on to refine the current system.

Wrapping Up

SAP implementation is probably the most challenging area to work in as a consultant. You are responsible for guiding your client through many of the potential pitfalls that exist and delivering a system that will replace existing legacy applications. This chapter has identified many of these critical areas and how you can better help your client and your own reputation with a successful SAP installation.

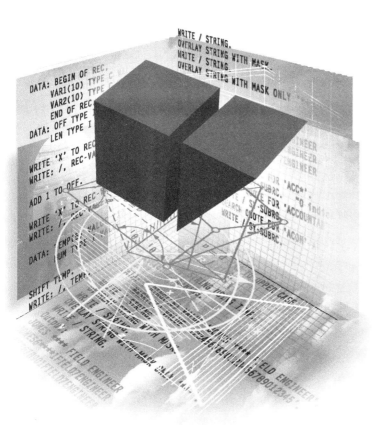

Chapter 16

Upgrades

Many aspects of an SAP upgrade are similar to a new installation of SAP. If you skipped Chapter 15, which discusses installing SAP, we encourage you to read it before proceeding. This chapter focuses on the differences between a new installation and an upgrade and on the areas to which the SAP professional should pay specific attention during an upgrade.

Upgrade Complexity

SAP upgrades vary in complexity. The factors that determine the amount of work to be done for the upgrade include:

- The difference in SAP release level
- The amount of new functionality the client wants to incorporate during the upgrade
- The amount and complexity of the modifications that were made to the original SAP installation
- How well documented the initial release was done with respect to customization settings in the IMG, interfaces, customer source code modifications, and bolt-on applications

If the client is moving from SAP R/3 version 2.2 to SAP R/3 version 4.0, you could be in for a significant amount of work. Each major release (2.x, 3.x, 4.x, etc.) of SAP usually includes new functionality, while the minor releases (3.1h, 4.0b, etc.) of SAP are usually reserved for product stability. In addition to the new functionality, there are also changes to existing SAP transactions. It's common for screens and fields to be renamed with a new release of SAP, causing additional work for programs that do Batch Data Communication (BDC) operations against these screens.

An upgrade of SAP is usually triggered by the desire of the client to get the latest features of SAP and to stay on a current version of SAP for supportability reasons. A common occurrence during upgrades is the urge to add new functionality to the existing SAP installation either due to the new features in the new release or simply because the upgrade will provide good opportunity to implement the new functions.

As mentioned in Chapter 15, "New Implementations," the entire business process must be analyzed to see what effect new functionality will have on the current procedures. If an upgrade is a purely technical upgrade (no installation of additional functionality), the upgrade team's staff can be reduced because little involvement is required from the business community.

TIP

It is important to keep the client aware of the additional complexity that adding new functionality will add. At the beginning of the upgrade project, criteria should be defined to determine whether a certain piece of new functionality should be added or not. Remember that a little technical change can make a big difference further down the business pipeline.

SAP provides the tools and instructions for upgrading from one release to another. If no direct source code modifications are made (i.e., without the use of transactions CMOD or SMOD) and all fields are used for their intended purpose, there would be little work for a consultant to do. The more modifications that have been made to the system, the longer the upgrade project will take. You have to be especially careful with clients that have allowed source code to be copied and then modified slightly. SAP cannot check for this kind of thing. If the original source code is modified during the upgrade (which is probable), then the modified code has to be updated as well. The problem is in finding all modules that were copied and modified.

The final factor that influences the amount of time that an upgrade will take is the level of documentation that has been kept on the original system. The documentation should describe the business rationale for all customizations and custom programs. Also, if the support documentation is kept current (see Chapter 17, "Support"), the team that is doing the upgrade will be able to understand why things are the way they are. If the documentation is not complete, the amount of time needed for upgrading increases because many areas have to be researched.

Depending on the original system installation, the number of changes to be made in the new installation, and past system maintenance and documentation, an SAP upgrade can take a great deal of time and resources.

Upgrading vs New Installation

An SAP upgrade is very similar to and just as challenging as a new installation. Upgrading includes determining what the new SAP functionality is and how it will fit into the current business plan, as well as setting up test plans, procedure documents, and the other documentation that is required. An upgrade, however, does have some significant differences when compared to a new installation.

The first major difference is that you have to deal with the existing SAP system. This involves more hardware while you are going through the development and testing phase since you must support both the old and new environments for the length of the upgrade. It also means that you have to incorporate changes made to the existing production environment into the upgraded system. The best way to handle this is to limit development of new functions, reports, and applications for the existing SAP system to critical problems only. Once you have started development on the upgraded system, bringing in transports from older systems can be a time-consuming task.

Depending on the new functionality that is added, there should be considerably less documentation done during an upgrade. Under ideal circumstances, the existing technical documentation need only be updated to account for changes in SAP. Usually the system-task documentation for the business users has to be reviewed to account for differences in button names and variations in menu paths, and new training documentation needs to be done to reflect any new screen layouts and functions.

Another difference between a new implementation and an upgrade is the level of experience of the people that you work with. You probably won't have to explain the simple aspects of SAP, and you should not have to deal with too many ABAP programmers with low levels of experience. The business analysis or functional side is also easier because the business users are familiar with SAP terminology and concepts. The analyst need only concentrate on business practices and settings for the new functionality to be implemented.

Another significant difference between upgrades and an original installation concerns undocumented source code changes, customizations, or copies of source code that are modified slightly. Finding these is difficult because you don't know where they are, and the changes may be very subtle and only occur under a very specific set of circumstances. It is very important when doing the preliminary work on an upgrade to ask as many people as you can about any source code changes, and to review existing documentation to determine if this problem exists. It is also important to try to find out as much background documentation as possible for the reasons behind the customization settings.

SAP Releases

SAP does a fairly good job of documenting the changes that are made in major and minor releases. This documentation can be found by clicking the Help menu on the toolbar (see Figure 16-1 and Figure 16-2).

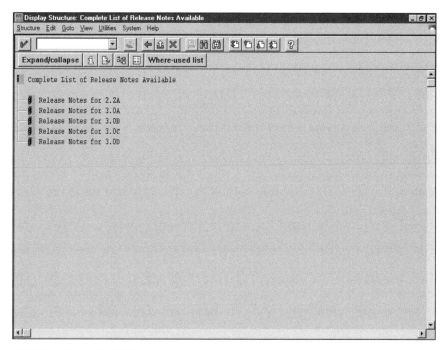

FIGURE 16-1 *The SAP release notes broken down per release*

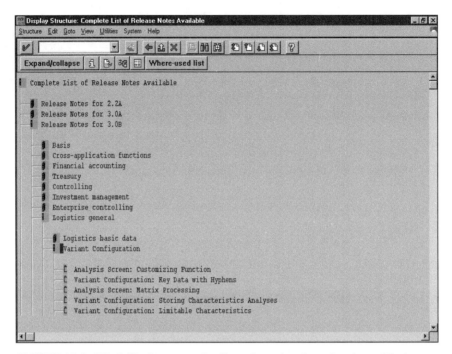

FIGURE 16-2 *The SAP release notes details can be used to determine the specific changes made in certain areas.*

SAP usually publishes release notes between major versions along with a new set for each minor release. So, if you are upgrading from a 3.1H to a 4.0C installation of SAP, you should review the 4.0 release notes as well as the 4.0B and 4.0C notes.

Reading through the notes is important, but it is also important to test any new functionality on the SAP system itself. The release notes often do not discuss all of the aspects of a new feature or change. Also, as with any new release, there is a new set of SAP bugs. Without testing, you will not know whether you have missed the application of the latest hot packages or OSS notes from SAP.

Beginning with release 4.0, SAP adopted a new strategy in which it will make one major release and one minor release per year. These releases will be denoted by an "A" for the major release and a "B" for the minor release. An example of this new naming convention is 4.5A for the major release and 4.5B for the minor release. As before, the major releases will contain the new functionality, and the minor releases will contain any patches that are required to make the new release more stable.

CAUTION

New major releases from SAP are usually fairly unstable and do not become stable until at least the "C" or "D" minor release is available. Some clients do not understand this and think that they can go live on, for example, release 4.0A, but this is not recommended. Though it is possible to go live on an early release, the cost is high in both tracking down bugs and in upgrading to the stable release.

Hardware Requirements

The recommended hardware architecture for any SAP implementation is to have a development system, a consolidation or test system, and a production system. Because it is very costly to have two development systems, two consolidation systems, and a production system during an upgrade, some clients may try to cut corners by combining one or more of these systems.

You should be aware of the hardware architecture that is currently in place and the changes that could occur to this architecture through the various stages of the upgrade. This includes the hardware and the operating system and database version on each machine.

Be sure that the development system is running the same version of SAP, database, and operating system as is the current production system so that support for the old production environment can be provided for as long as possible. Ideally, this development environment will be available until the upgrade takes place.

Develop a Disaster Recovery Plan (DRP). After you have a complete understanding of how the architecture will look during all phases of the upgrade (including the upgrade process itself), think about how you would recover if the production system had a critical failure. Things to consider include the amount of time it would take to get a production system back online and what kind of throughput (both speed and storage-wise) it would have.

At a minimum, be sure that the final test of the upgrade is a complete test and done on a system that has approximately the same performance statistics as the production environment. Ideally, this is done well in advance of the actual upgrade, because it is here that you can determine whether there are any database sizing issues (both in the areas of tablespace and physical drive space) or any performance-related problems that occur because of the upgrade. You will also be

---

Code Synchronization

Code and customization synchronization between the two development systems (one for the production system and the other used for the upgrade) is usually a problem during upgrades. It is very important to limit the number of changes done to the production environment during the upgrade project. All changes that were made to support the current production environment also need to be brought into the upgrade systems, and this could take a considerable amount of time to resolve. There is also the possibility of missing some of the changes.

---

able to see if any of the functionality and customization has interfered with any other application or process.

The Upgrade

The general steps to take for an SAP system upgrade are listed below. Compare this plan to the plan at your current client to ensure that critical steps are not missed:

◆ Verify that the original SAP system is functioning properly, check system logs, job logs, and database logs

◆ Get a full system backup of the original SAP system

◆ Ensure that there is adequate tablespace and disk space for the upgrade

◆ Lock down users during the upgrade process

◆ Cancel all released background jobs in SAP and any job on the operating system that may affect the upgrade

◆ Carry out database-specific preparations; i.e., disable archiving

◆ Begin the upgrade by using the SAP upgrade, database, and language CDs

◆ Regenerate all programs using RSREGEN

◆ Bring up the system and verify the installation

◆ Apply all necessary hot packages

♦ Apply all transports for customer code and modifications

♦ Perform a full backup of the system, including the database

♦ Run all jobs to process data that has gathered during the upgrade

♦ Reschedule jobs

♦ Unlock users

Immediately after the upgrade, the consolidation and development systems should be ready to support the new production environment. Nearly all upgrades require at least a few quick code fixes and customization settings to be sent to the production system within the first 12 to 24 hours of going live.

TIP

Before making direct updates to SAP code, look through the CMOD or SMOD transactions to see whether SAP has provided a new user exit that can be used instead of a direct source code modification. See SAP's online help for more details on these transactions and on how to perform customer modifications.

NOTE

New development that is done during an upgrade should follow the same procedures as outlined in Chapter 15, with specific attention paid to how the new development will affect other business processes.

OSS Notes

You should ensure that all OSS Notes that pertain to your client's SAP installation are applied. This is especially true when trying to go live on an early version of a major release. Although SAP provides hot packages to apply critical OSS notes, these do not always include the more subtle notes that could affect your site.

Figure 16-3 shows the OSS system search screen. Each week before the upgrade, do a search through the system to see if all pertinent OSS notes have been applied for your site.

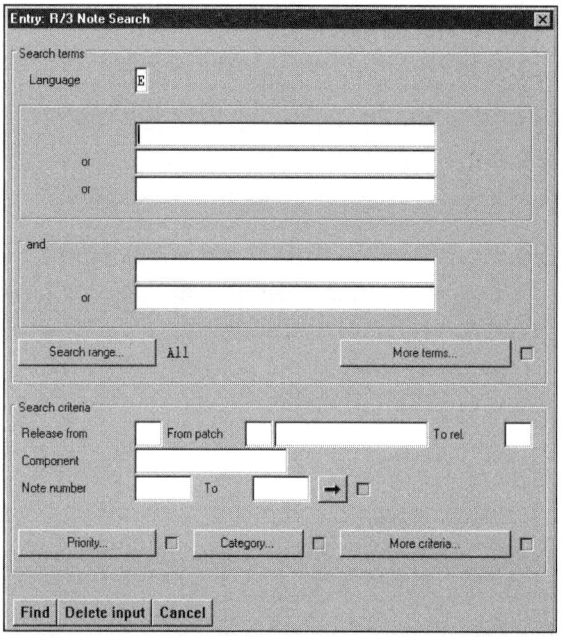

FIGURE 16-3 *The OSS System Entry R/3 Note Search screen, where you define the criteria that you want to look for OSS Notes*

Testing

The testing phase on an SAP upgrade generally follows the same pattern as the testing phase for a new implementation. It is important to ensure that security profiles for model users are tested so that the model user can perform just the tasks that they are supposed to. This is an area that SAP does not document well in its release notes and is a typical problem for upgrades that are not well-tested.

Also, be sure that testing does not affect production in any way. For instance, be sure that documents printed during the test are not confused with real documents printed from the production SAP system. This also applies to outgoing data interfaces.

Training and Documentation

The amount of training involved during an upgrade is usually considerably less than that of a new installation. Typically all that needs to be done is a brief tour for the users of the new functionality and any changes that may have occurred in the menu paths, buttons, and reporting features.

One area that must be carefully examined is business procedure documentation, which business users follow as step-by-step instructions for their specific tasks within SAP. This documentation must be carefully scrutinized to make sure that all of the correct menu paths, buttons, fields names, and so forth are correct for the new version of SAP. Be sure to schedule enough time for this task, as it can take a while to gather all of the original documentation and go through it page-by-page.

Wrapping Up

Working through an SAP upgrade is challenging. Depending on the project, the SAP upgrade can be straightforward and quick, or it can last longer than the initial release of the SAP system. As an SAP professional on an upgrade project, you need to ensure that the client has an adequate DRP, that all source code modifications are updated, and that adequate testing and documentation is done before the actual upgrade occurs. All of these steps will ensure that new business functionality integrates smoothly into the existing system, and that the team of people that will be supporting the system after the upgrade will be able to do so without having to do a lot of cleanup work in the areas of code, training, and documentation.

Chapter 17

Support

The knowledge and skills needed to provide ongoing support and solve the client's day-to-day problems are different than those the consultant or a permanent employee needs to do for an initial SAP installation or upgrade. Support should not be provided solely by programmers, but by a combination of programmers and business analysts.

Troubleshooting Techniques

One function of working in a support position is to troubleshoot problems as they arise. Some of the techniques that we apply when determining the cause of the problems are:

◆ **Quickly scan the system.** Pay attention to anything that may be related to the specific area that you are trying to troubleshoot. See "System Surfing" later in this chapter.

◆ **Check less obvious places.** In addition to the transactions used to scan the system, the system log can provide a wealth of information on the exact sequence of events (see Figure 17-1).

◆ **Try to recreate the problem on a test or consolidation system.** If the problem can be repeated or re-created, run either a run-time analysis or a trace. These tools can indicate the path the program is taking or the data that it is trying to retrieve/store.

◆ **Try to find where the SAP error message is located.** Start the transaction, enter debug mode, and then put a breakpoint in for the keyword **message**. Another way is to do a *where-used* on the message number itself.

◆ **Check the SAP OSS system for the same type of problem.** If you have determined which program, include, or function module is causing the problem, look up all OSS notes using these as key words. Many times the keys used in OSS are not very clear, but SAP usually enters the name of the ABAP function that is affected.

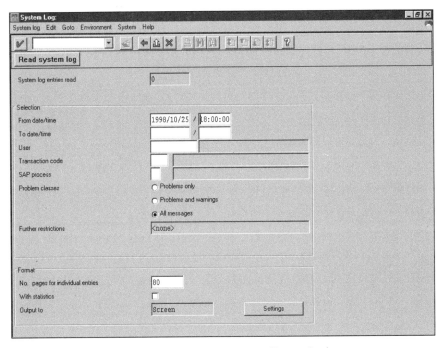

FIGURE 17-1 *An example of the transaction SM21 (System Log)*

◆ **Determine whether anything changed on the production system just before the problem occurred.** Look at transports going into the production system for both code and customizations that could cause the problem.

◆ **If all else fails.** Either enter debug mode and do a single-step analysis through the code (usually many times) until you determine what the problem is, or log an OSS note with SAP.

Bolt-on Applications and Table Extensions

Although you may have a great deal of experience in SAP, nothing quite prepares you for what a client may have added as a bolt-on application or for the modifications that the client has made to SAP code and tables.

If you don't know it's there, you can't update it!

A client may have created a new table to contain information related to a standard SAP table instead of extending the table definition. There may be no practical way to determine this relationship on your own, and you may write programs to update/add/delete records from the SAP table without taking into account the bolt-on table. Always make sure that any code changes you propose or make are reviewed by someone who has experience at this specific client site and has knowledge of the client's specific changes.

 CAUTION

When working with any program or data, it is important to discuss the solution or modification that you are planning with a person who has worked in this functional area for some time. If this cannot be done, extreme care should be taken to ensure that all bolt-on or database modifications are taken into consideration.

Critical Jobs

One of the first things that must be determined when providing support for a client is which are the critical jobs or programs that must be executed for the area that you are supporting. Critical jobs are those jobs that will stop the business from functioning if they do not run.

Learn these jobs and their associated programs well. Understand or know about each of the following for each job that you are responsible for:

- ◆ The purpose of each step of the job
- ◆ The schedule the job runs on, or what other job or event triggers it to run
- ◆ If there are any jobs or events that are dependent on this job's completion
- ◆ All associated inbound and outbound files, and where backups are stored
- ◆ Recover procedures
- ◆ Who or which department to contact if there is a problem

Make sure that there is a monitoring system in place that alerts you if a critical job stops or is cancelled. This can be a manual system of logging on to the system and scanning through completed jobs, or having a monitor program run and page you if a specific job aborts.

 TIP

If you are responsible for several jobs scheduled in SAP, try to have all of them run under a single background user ID. This will help you when scanning for all of your jobs.

When first starting to support a job, it is a good idea to locate any documentation that exists for it. Make sure that you have at least a high level data flow diagram which shows all of the various files and other data sources and how they interact with the programs. If you cannot find such a document, make one. The more complicated the job, the more important this diagram is.

If you are responsible for monitoring a critical job, ensure that if you go on vacation or are absent from the workplace for a few days, there is adequate knowledge transfer to the person who will be monitoring the job in your place. Make sure that items specific to you, such as e-mail addresses and pager numbers, are either changed or accessible by this person.

Data Integrity

When working with data, do not assume that the only values in a field are those of the check table. Over time, people who do not know any better may delete entries from the check tables without removing or converting the associated tables. One of your tasks as a support consultant is to ensure that the data in SAP remains clean.

 CAUTION

Never remove a value from any customization table without first checking all tables that have a field that could have this value. You must find out what to do with these records before changing the customization.

TIP

SAP is an integrated system. If you are working with the Material Master, which remains relatively static, and by accident you mess up the database, you cannot simply restore it. Transactions such as purchase orders and sales orders are constantly entering the system and referencing this data.

New Development

There are a few differences between doing development work in a support environment and doing a new installation or an upgrade of SAP. These differences hinge on ensuring that the data integrity is maintained in the production environment.

Prior to starting a new development, ask your client if and when the client is planning on upgrading to a newer version of SAP. Any new development should be compatible with any new functionality that may be coming out in SAP (see SAP's Web site, **www.sap.com**).

You need to go through the usual design process and ensure that there is a support environment for the existing environment and a development environment for the new solution. Unlike a real upgrade, you do not have additional hardware, so you need the current and new systems to work together or stage the release of the new functionality. You also need to ensure that things such as table extensions are brought in properly to the production environment. An extension to the Sales Order or Material Master can lock up the database for several minutes or even longer as it is being generated to incorporate the new structure. This can have adverse affects on other jobs.

Depending on the types of new developments, there may also be issues of backfilling old data and synchronizing training and documentation to correspond to the changes that occur to the production environment. You must ensure that people still get adequate training and documentation for the old system until the new system is in place.

System Surfing

Checking on the overall status of the system is the job of the Basis consultant or infrastructure team. However, ABAP programmers and other support personnel can also help make sure that the system is running smoothly.

You should do the following on a regular basis:

◆ **Background Job Overview.** Check all jobs that you are responsible for to see if any have been canceled or if they are taking longer than expected (see Figure 17-2).

◆ **SAP Enqueue locks.** Through transaction SM12, check to ensure that there are no stale locks (locks that have been there for more than a few hours. See Figure 17-3).

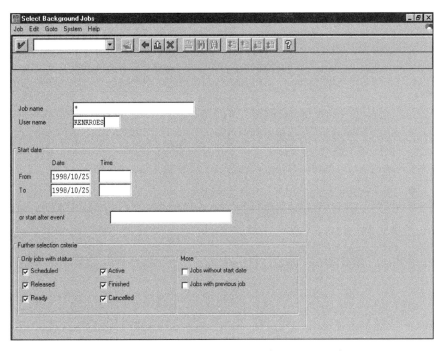

FIGURE 17-2 *An example of the transaction SM37 (Job Overview)*

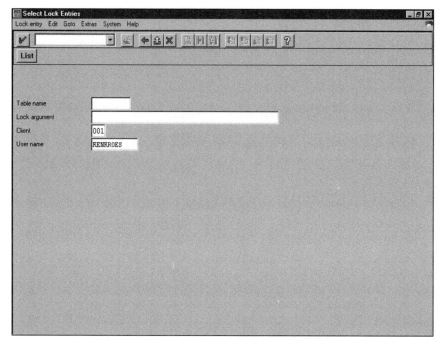

FIGURE 17-3 *An example of the transaction SM12 (Enqueue Locks)*

◆ **Database size and fragmentation.** Take the tables that are most often used in your area and make sure that there is enough space and that they are not too badly fragmented (see Figure 17-4).

◆ **Dump Analysis.** Check whether any dumps have occurred in the past few days through transaction ST22. Determine the cause for the dumps. For example, a report that users run online takes too long and dumps because it exceeds the maximum time allowed (see Figure 17-5). You can also get valuable information from variables such as the current record being accessed from the database.

◆ **Update Analysis.** Ensure that no steps are waiting to finish in an update task. Anything waiting for more than one hour should be checked (see Figure 17-6).

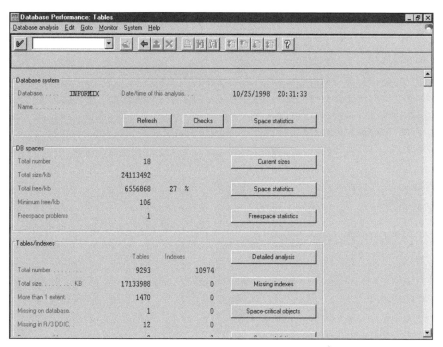

FIGURE 17-4 *An example of the transaction DB02 (Database Analysis)*

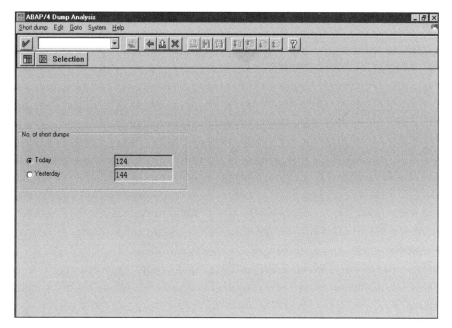

FIGURE 17-5 *An example of the transaction ST22 (Dump Analysis)*

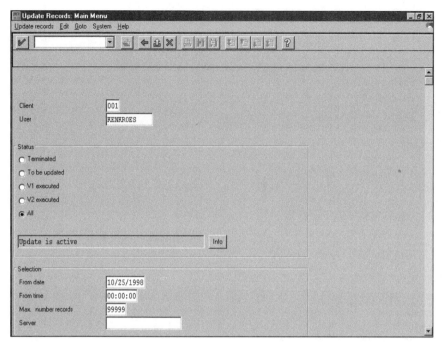

FIGURE 17-6 *An example of the transaction SM13 (Update Analysis)*

Working with Users

A good support consultant has excellent rapport with the user community that he or she is supporting. You need to be able to help them out of problems that they get into, provide them with information and training, and develop new programs that will make their jobs more efficient. Building a rapport with the end-user community is done through showing genuine concern that you want to make their job easier and delivering high-quality work on schedule.

You must, however, be very careful when dealing directly with users of the system. First, you are usually not the person responsible for business decisions. If a user asks you a question that involves a business process and you are not the person that is responsible for this process, you should point that person back to their supervisor or manager. Also, be careful about modifying data on the system. As a support SAP consultant, you will have a significant level of access to the production environment. It is easy for you to change a vendor's address or material description. Unless absolutely necessary, you should avoid data modification; leave it to the normal business process.

Documentation

Each client has its own expectations regarding the level of documentation that should be provided for work that is performed on either existing or new programs, but it is your job to ensure that the documentation is easily found and is useful.

Updating initial design documentation is a waste of time. Keeping the initial design document current takes considerable effort, even for minor changes, and the chances of forgetting to update areas in the documentation are quite high.

There are two methods for documenting changes to existing programs. The first is to make revision documents. With this approach, the original design document is left intact and a new document is written that specifically outlines the changes that are made. A revision list, which can be included in the original document, is then maintained and lists all of these revision documents.

A better method is to create and maintain a living support document for the solution (see "Living Documentation" in Chapter 12). The living support document contains:

- ◆ A general data flow diagram
- ◆ Location of design and any related business procedure documentation
- ◆ Recovery instructions for the solution
- ◆ Input and output file movements
- ◆ Development class, transaction names, and major tables used

It is also very important to update user or business procedures that may be affected by any change made to the programs. The user or business procedures are usually correct when SAP is first installed, but they have a habit of becoming out-of-date a few years after the installation. This includes not only the written documentation, but also customization notes in the IMG and online documentation available through the client intranet site.

Wrapping Up

The job of a support consultant is very different from that of working on a project to install or upgrade SAP. The support consultant must be able to troubleshoot production problems quickly, ensure database integrity, keep documentation up-to-date, and build a rapport with the user community that he or she is supporting. This type of consulting can also be detrimental, as the consultant can lose touch with the latest SAP developments and decrease their marketability. It is vital to keep current on the latest that SAP has to offer.

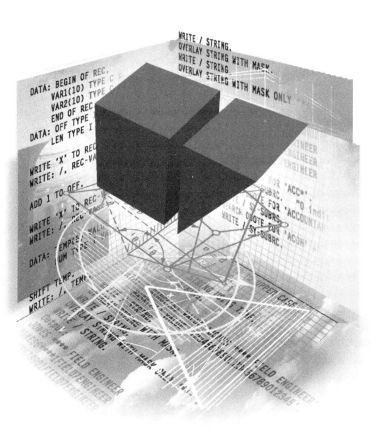

Chapter 18

Design

During each phase of an implementation, you will play different roles as an SAP professional. In this chapter, you'll cover the design phases for implementing a specific solution or project within SAP, and you'll review the various points of problem analysis, design, construction, testing, and implementation.

Problem Analysis

When given the task of implementing a solution, the most important part of the entire design process is the analysis of the problem. SAP is an integrated system, and any modification or addition to a program, database table, or customization can affect all areas of a business. The more you understand how your job impacts other areas, the better your solution will be. This design process can take as little as one hour in a meeting for a simple new report, or up to several years for a full-blown SAP implementation.

Understanding the Situation

The first step in problem analysis in SAP is understanding how the new solution fits into the current environment. If you are asked to add a field to an existing SAP table, determine which programs and processes use this table and how your change may affect them. If your task is to implement a whole SAP module, the analysis focuses on how this module integrates with all other SAP modules, along with any legacy systems. For large implementations, functional analysts must work as a team to understand how the client needs to have the SAP system configured. Understanding the bigger picture involves meeting with the people that will be affected by any change to determine exactly what impact the solution will have. The size of the change does not matter, since adding just a field to an SAP table will make an impact.

During this phase it is important to identify business owners for all data fields and processes that will be stored and used. Data fields that do not have a clearly defined owner can sometimes be used for different things by different areas, which can lead to confusion and corrupt data. Data ownership usually can be determined by finding out who or what group designates the acceptable values for a data field (i.e., check tables).

Technical Issues

The second step of problem analysis is to look at the technical issues. Some of the questions raised in this process should be the following:

- ◆ Are there legacy systems that need to be interfaced with?
- ◆ Are new reports required?
- ◆ How current does the data have to be?
- ◆ Is a transaction needed? Is Internet access needed?
- ◆ Is access to this data to be restricted?

The technical issue phase is a very important step of the problem analysis for any solution. Doing this step thoroughly usually leads to a successful implementation of the solution; on the other hand, not doing a proper problem analysis leads to either a failed solution, or one that takes much longer than necessary to implement.

Initial Design and Review

The initial design and review stage of a project is where a rough solution is drafted and presented to the business areas. When building the draft of the solution, do not dwell on the technical issues. Concentrate instead on the data flow and how the data is going to be entered, moved, deleted, and so forth.

Once the draft solution is prepared, have a working session with both the business community and technical staff to discuss whether the solution is plausible or if it could be improved upon. There may be several iterations of this phase until a solution is agreed upon both by the business and technical areas.

If the solution is large, it may help to mock up a simulated system with SAP to better show the final result. This can also help in uncovering design problems because of limitations and restrictions within SAP.

Detail Design

Detail design is the phase where all technical aspects of your project are written out. Detail design includes data flow diagrams, customization requirements, report outlines and storage requirements. Some of the more technical issues are discussed next.

SAP Table Design

Follow these rules when creating or modifying tables within SAP:

♦ **Identify an owner.** For each field that will contain data input from either a user or interface, excluding technical fields such as time stamps and internal indexes, an owner must be identified. This owner (which may be an entire business group) will be responsible for defining what will be going into the field, how it will be populated, and the contents of any check table that may be used. Failure to identify a single owner for a field will cause problems later, as there will always be confusion or debate on how a particular field is to be used.

♦ **Use one distinct piece of data per field.** Do not overload database fields; for example, a field that contains both a company name and location should be divided into two fields, one for the name and one for the location.

♦ **Put check tables (customization) everywhere possible.** Do not allow any hard-coded checks for data in programs.

♦ **Consider how the data will eventually be deleted and how the new table/field will work with SAP's current data archival project.** The solution may simply be a program to delete any records that are more than a certain number of days old, or you may need to place a deletion indicator in the table. Also, consider how your project is impacted if other SAP source data is deleted. For example, if the material master record is deleted and your table relates to the material, will it still work? Should it be archived at the same time? Should the existence of your record prevent the material master record from being archived?

♦ **Take notice of all secondary indices that are set up.** Secondary indices allow for faster database access but also take up valuable system resources when data is stored or modified.

◆ **Consider how the table/field will initially be populated.** It is poor practice to not backfill data and wait for the data to populate slowly over time. For instance, if you have a bolt-on table for the vendor master, all vendors should have their entries updated at once instead of having the vendors updated only when their master data is changed.

Source Code Modifications

SAP has made several areas of its programs easy to customize for a specific customer. These are identified through the transaction CMOD (see Figure 18-1) or SMOD (see Figure 18-2). This allows user-specific code to be placed at predefined points of an SAP process. For instance, you can place a user exit at the end of the saving of a purchase order, which might update a new bolt-on table. Modifications done through CMOD or SMOD survive SAP upgrades.

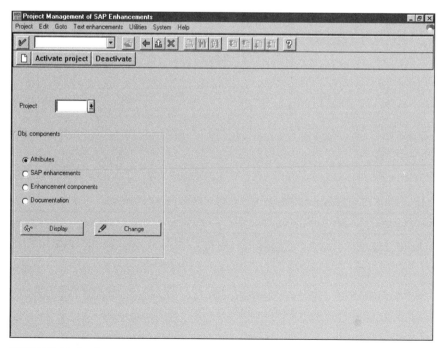

FIGURE 18-1 *An example of the transaction CMOD.*

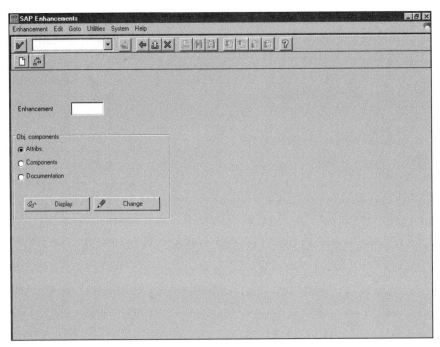

FIGURE 18-2 *An example of the transaction SMOD.*

SAP Enhancements through the transaction CMOD and SMOD are not limited to code modifications. Through this transaction, you can also modify field descriptions, transactions, menus, screen dynpros, and function module exits (see Table 18-1).

Table 18-1 SAP Enhancements per Development Class

Description	Dev. Class	# of Enhanc.
Temporary objects, never transported!	$TMP	1
Assets: Master Data	AA	6
Asset Accounting	AB	2
Asset Accounting kernel	ABAS	3
Simple cap. investment projects	AIP	1
Asset Accounting reporting	AR	2

Table 18-1 SAP Enhancements per Development Class *(continued)*

Description	Dev. Class	# of Enhanc.
Application Link Enabling	BALE	2
Customizing R/3 general table settings	BCUC	6
Service master: basic data	BDAS	1
Information System	BRST	1
R/3 Application development:		
PP Product Costing	CK	1
PS Basic data	CN	10
Structure	CNIS	1
PP Production orders	CO	3
PP Orders Process Orders	COCR	2
PP Task Lists	CP	2
PP Bills of Material	CS	3
Resource Planning	CY01	2
Archiving for application area PP	CORE	1
Characteristics	CT	1
Variant configuration	CU	2
Financial accounting 'Basis'	FBAS	10
Customers	FBD	2
Vendors	FBK	2
Dunning	FBM	1
G/L Accounts	FBS	1
Payments	FBZ	13
Consolidation	FK	1
R/3 customizing for Treasury bank and treasury functions	FTEC	5
Interface to external systems for tax Calculation	FYTX	1
FI-SL Customizing/integration/Basis	GBAS	1
Application Development R/3 Batch Input for PM	IBIP	1
R/3 Customer Service	ICSV	5
Application Development R/3 Equipment Management	IEQM	2

Table 18-1 SAP Enhancements per Development Class (continued)

Description	Dev. Class	# of Enhanc.
Appl. Development R/3 Plant Maintenance:		
Order Processing	IWO1	2
Order History	IWO2	1
Application Development R/3 Work Order Cycle	IWOC	1
Cost Accounting reporting, PMS RK-M	KAHF	6
Cost Accounting, Orders	KAUF	2
Cost Accounting Controlling EIS	KC	4
Profitability Analysis	KE	2
Profit Center Accounting	KE1	2
Period costing individual case	KKAG	1
Cost Accounting unit costing	KKEK	1
Integration CO/SD	KSDI	1
Interfaces	LVS	28
Application development R/3:		
Inventory management	MB	2
Inventory Controlling	MCB	1
Purchasing Information System	MCE	1
Shop Floor Information System	MCF	1
Sales & Operations Planning	MCP2	4
Logistics Info Sys. (Reporting)	MCR	3
Logistics Information Warehouse	MCS	1
Sales Information System	MCV	3
LIS: Early Warning	MCY	2
Appl. development R/3 MPS/determin.		
requirements planning	MD03	2
Evaluation	MD05	2
Application development R/3 purchasing	MDPB	1
Vendors/Material Relationships & Cond.	ME	10
Vendor evaluation	MEL	1

Table 18-1 SAP Enhancements per Development Class *(continued)*

Description	Dev. Class	# of Enhanc.
Application development R/3 dist. material master AL	MGV	1
R/3 services management	ML	2
Incoming invoices	MR	3
Appl. development R/3 decentralized invoice verification	MRM	1
Development of the R/3 HR application for master data	PBAS	2
Incentive Wages	PINW	1
Development of the R/3 time management Application	PTIM	6
Application development R/3:		
QM master Data	QA	4
QM in Procurement	QB	5
QM Certificates	QC	3
QM sample determination	QDSE	5
QM results recording	QE	15
QM interfaces insp. Processing	QEIF	16
QM inspection lot	QL	4
QM inspection specifications	QM	2
QM inspection plan characteristics	QP	6
quality notifications	QQM	8
QM reorganization of trans. Data	QR02	1
QM in sales and distribution	QS	3
QM usage decision	QV	7
Documentation: Interactive programming	SAB5	58
ABAP/4 runtime environment	SABP	2
Demo objects	SBCS	1
Screen Painter	SCRP	1
ABAP/4 Development Workbench:		
BEAC Corporate Flight System	SDW5	1
DDIC editor	SEDD	1
Program editor	SEDI	1

Table 18-1 SAP Enhancements per Development Class *(continued)*

Description	Dev. Class	# of Enhanc.
ABAP/4 Development Workbench	SEU	4
'Small editors' and development environment	SEUA	2
Menu Painter	SEUC	4
Function library	SFCS	1
ABAP/4 Reporting	SM38	2
Dynamic menu	SMEN	4
SAPoffice	SO	1
R/3 applications development:		
ABAP/4 Query	SQUE	1
User master	SUSR	1
R/3 central Basis development:		
Address management	SZAD	1
Date calendar	SZTK	2
Application development R/3 sales	VA	1
ALE development in sales and Distribution	VALE	1
Application development R/3:		
Batch Determination	VB	1
CAS – activities	VCA	5
Application development R/3:		
EDI	VED	5
foreign trade	VEI	1
invoice	VF	7
shipping	VL	4
SD master data distribution	VSV	1
SD R/3 transport processing	VTR	1
Application development R/3 RV central functions	VZ	1
IS-R: Replenishment list	WBBC	1
IS-R: POS interface	WPOS	2

Screen Design

It is important to do a rough draft of all of the screens that are to be developed and to discuss the screens with the business area that will be using them. When the business area is presented with a visual representation of what they will be seeing (i.e., your screen outlines), it may help them to visualize how the whole design will work.

 CAUTION

When you design screens that represent data, be careful about using colors, which may confuse people who are color-blind.

After the initial screen drafts are done, run them past an ABAP programmer to make sure that they are BDC-friendly. For instance, there is often a problem when there is a scrollable list on the screen where a user must select a line to view the detail behind it. In this instance, make sure that there is a function to position the selectable line.

Report Design

If your project involves many reports that will all be doing the same kind of selects, consider having a periodic job run to gather this information once and place it into a temporary table (e.g., the cluster table INDX). This will avoid wasting system resources to do the same thing with many reports.

Instead of making several similar reports for users' different needs, make one report with options on it. This reduces the coding time and makes maintenance much easier.

Make sure that you consider the potential run-times of reports. Any report that could take more than a few minutes to run online should be designed to run as a background report that the user views when it is finished. This means that the user should be able to enter all of his or her data on the first screen and then submit the job for background processing, instead of entering some data, executing the program, then entering some more refinements and running the program again to get more detail.

Interface Design

Interface design covers programs that will either read in data from other systems or send data out to other systems. Make sure that the design includes recovery procedures. For example, if the database server goes down in the middle of an interface run, there should be a graceful way to restart the interface without data loss. Many designs do not initially consider this.

Interfaces should also be designed to handle errors gracefully. This means that the person who is responsible for the interface execution will not have to do a great amount of work when an error is encountered. One way to do this is to store the inbound record(s) in a transparent table if they error out, and then have the user select the records and press a button to have them run through the interface software again.

Most inbound interfaces for SAP write out BDC sessions, which are then processed through the appropriate transactions. A well-designed interface considers possible changes to the customizations and how they can affect screen and data flow.

ABAP Design

There are many design considerations to take into account that are purely ABAP related and that affect Report, Interface, and Transaction work. Near the beginning of the design process, consider these matters:

◆ **Determine all LUWs (Logical Units of Work) that are to occur for the process.** The LUWs drive how the transactions and interfaces will be written. A logical unit of work is all of the data that must be stored together to represent one business transaction or one master record.

◆ **Plan security authorization at the onset of all ABAP design.** When setting up the authorizations, make sure you set up who will be responsible for assigning these authorizations to the users.

Customizations

As part of the design process, set up maintenance transactions for each customization table, make sure the proper security authorization is set up, and determine the method of table population (directly on the production system or through transport). Then set up the customization interface through the IMG and include notes on what and why the changes to the customizations were made. The new customization table procedure follows:

1. Build up the transaction to maintain the table.
2. Make sure the security is correct for table access.
3. Determine if the table entries will be modified directly or transported.
4. Document the solution.

Construction

Once the design phase has been completed and approved, it is time to start the construction phase of the project. Key points for the construction phase are:

◆ Ensure that all programmers working on the solution adhere to the same standards and guidelines.

◆ Once there is a buy-off on the initial design, the design should be frozen and changes to the initial design should be made only under controlled circumstances. The people requesting the change and the business owners of your project need to be made aware of the impact of any changes before the change is accepted.

◆ For projects where the construction period takes a significant amount of time, keep your project owners abreast of how the work is coming and inform them well in advance if you expect that there will be delays.

◆ The construction phase includes all of the support documentation required for the solution and any other documentation that the client requires.

Testing

Though the programming staff should do the initial testing of a project, another party should perform the final testing of the project. When a bug is found and fixed, an evaluation should be done to see what other functionality could be affected by the bug's fix. These areas need to be retested.

When setting up test scenarios, ensure that there is complete end-to-end testing with your new solution, as well as with any other solution that your project needs to interface with. Though your solution may test well, a mistake may have been made in the interface design, and the error wouldn't appear until the whole process is tested. The testing should also ensure that the documentation for both support and business are correct.

Training

Depending on the type of solution that is being designed, there are basically two different groups that need to be trained. The first group is the end-users or the people that will be using the solution or the data from the solution.

The second group is the support staff. They will have to understand the various customizations, data relationships, and programs. Interfaces need support staff that understand how to monitor and recover the jobs. Make sure that the staff knows where the support documentation can be found.

Implementation

A successful implementation is problem free. Depending on what is being installed on the production system, you may want several practice runs to ensure that everything goes well for the real thing.

If your solution involves the modification of existing data in SAP, ensure that you have a plan in place in case there is a problem halfway through and you need to get back to the original data. Also, go through your implementation plan with the business area to make sure that it understands and approves anything that may affect the business area during implementation.

Wrapping Up

Due to the integrated environment, SAP can be a difficult area in which to do development. For any project, extra care must be taken during the problem analysis phase to ensure that all business angles are covered. Care should also be taken in all phases of design to make the solution as easy as possible to develop and maintain. Construction and testing of any project should adhere to specific rules, which will lead to a smooth installation.

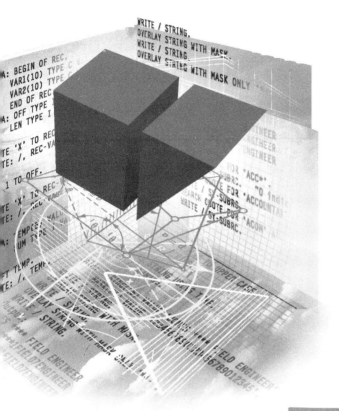

PART IV

Appendixes

A   *SAP Internet Resources*

B   *Per Diem Rates*

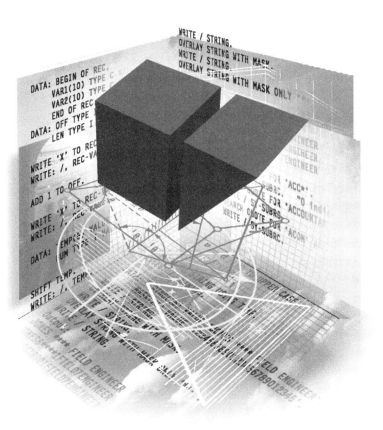

Appendix A

**SAP Internet
Resources**

The Internet is a valuable source of information for new contracts, information about SAP, and the ERP industry in general for an SAP consultant. Information provided by the Internet contains both national and international content. Part of the problem with the Internet, however, is finding reliable information quickly. Doing even sophisticated searches such as "+SAP +SUPPLY +CHAIN +CONTRACT" with Web search engines such as Excite, Lycos, or Yahoo leads to hundreds of links, most of which do not contain the information you seek. The following is a collection of sites that we frequent with useful content.

Job Sites

The SAP Career Center for Allen Davis & Associates (**www.softwarejobs.com/ sapbody.html**) is loaded with available positions as well as many well-written articles on SAP and consulting. There are a variety of links from this page to other SAP-related sites, including the ERP News Center, which is a collection of categorized articles on the latest developments in SAP, PeopleSoft, and Supply Chain. You may also subscribe to a weekly e-mailing of their *Opportunities in SAP* newsletter.

Based in Atlanta, ACSYS IT (**www.acsysit.com**) is a premier SAP implementation partner that provides functional and technical consulting, implementation, and post-implementation services to FORTUNE 500 clients. With over $40 million in annual revenues, ACSYS IT is a National SAP Implementation Partner. ACSYS IT offers end-to-end SAP R/3 implementation solutions using the ASAP methodology for all core modules, and specializes in the Finance and Logistics, Human Resources, and Business Information Warehouse modules.

The Web page for SAPient ES, Inc. (**www.sap-contracting.com/sap.htm**) has a great deal of information on SAP links and, of course, job postings.

Based out of Canada, Upgradables Plus (**www.upgradablesplus.com/index.htm**) is an information systems integration company that provides worldwide consulting services in SAP solutions. Its Web site contains a good job posting search engine, which is divided by functional area.

JobSite (**www.jobsite.co.uk/**) contains thousands of live job vacancies from Europe's leading recruitment agencies and direct employers. Vacancies are only displayed for one week, so no time is wasted applying for jobs that have already been filled.

Dice.com (**www.dice.com/**) is a job search Web site for all computer professionals. Dice.com lists thousands of high-tech permanent, contract, and consulting jobs nationwide (United States). Go straight to the advanced job search to save time. The advanced job search allows you to look specifically for various types of contract positions (W2 or independent).

JOBfind (**www.jobfind.com.au**) is another general job bank based in Australia. JOBfind contains a lot of listings for SAP work for around the world, but is primarily focused on Australia.

JOBNET (**www.jobnet.com.au**) is a job bank for computer professionals and has one of the largest collection of jobs for Australia, New Zealand, and Asia.

SAP Information

The SAPFAQ page (**www.sapfaq.com**) is a very good site for information on SAP, with lots of links to other sites. Topics covered include basic information on SAP, information on R/2 and R/3, ABAP, book reviews, user groups, training, and more.

Although the ERPSuperSite (**www.erpsupersite.com/**) is not specifically for SAP, it is a very good site on Enterprise Resource Planning Software, providing loads of links to related articles. As a consultant, it is vital that you keep abreast of where the market is going. We visit this site every few weeks to find out the latest.

The SAP Info Web site (**www.sapinfo.com/**) has lots of information on SAP through its forums and mailing lists. It also has basic information on SAP, book reviews, and job opportunities.

The SAP Resource Centre (**src.thehub.com.au/**) contains many good pages of information on SAP and consulting in the SAP world. There is also a very good set of links to national and international consulting agencies.

The Advanced Guide to Implementing ALE (**www.geocities.com/SiliconValley/ Foothills/8207/index.htm**) is an excellent site for information regarding Application Link Enabling (ALE), and it has some very useful links to worldwide job opportunities.

IT Toolset for SAP (www.sapassist.com/) is part of a collection from erpassist.com, which also has sites for BAAN, Oracle, and PeopleSoft, as well as a general site related to ERP. This site has a very good knowledge base along with sections on recruiting and forums to discuss ERP topics. What really impresses us about this site is its extensive set of SAP-related links, which are nicely grouped together in areas such as "SAP News and Press Releases," "SAP Training," "Third Party Products," "SAP Recruiters," and more.

SAP Sites

SAP's home page (www.sap.com/) is a good source for general information and for finding out what new features are soon to be released. It also has schedules for SAP conferences such as Sapphire. You can also sign up for the free e-mail newsletter, "SAP Flash."

SAP's SAPNet (www.sap-ag.de/saphelp.htm) requires an OSS logon. This site has loads of information from SAP. There are chat networks and forums, articles regarding new technologies, OSS and SSCR functionality, downloadable documentation, and more.

SAP Labs, Inc. (formerly SAP Technology, Inc.) (www.saplabs.com/saplabhm. htm) develops cutting-edge software and add-ons for the SAP R/3 System. They are an extension of the R/3 System development group located in Walldorf, Germany. This site has information about their company, SAP, and job opportunities.

SAP User Groups

ASUG (Americas' SAP Users' Group) (www.asug.com) is an independent, non-profit organization of SAP customer companies and eligible third-party vendors and consultants.

A discussion group for SAP software is located at **www.realtime-usa.com/sap-group/**. There are archives on discussions as far back as 1996.

The SAP-R3-L list is for discussion of SAP's R/3 software. To find out about the list and how it operates, send an e-mail to **LISTSERV@MITVMA.MIT.EDU** with INFO SAP-R3-L as the first line of the body of the message. Additional information can be obtained by including as the second line in the same message (or as the first line in a separate message to the same address) GET SAP-R3-L WELCOME.

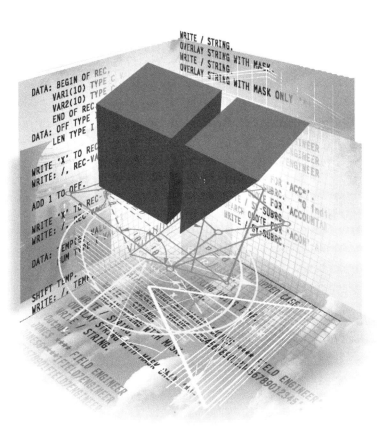

Appendix B

Per Diem Rates

United States Per Diem Rates

The following are selected per diem rates for the United States, taken from the federal government Web site (**policyworks.gov/org/main/mt/**).

Rates vary by state and city and by time of year. You should ensure that you have current values before entering into any contract (see Table B-1).

Table B-1 Sampling of Per Diem Rates in the United States (Aug. 1998) in Dollars

Location	Lodging	Food	Total
Standard rate	50	30	80
ALABAMA			
Birmingham	64	38	102
Montgomery	67	30	97
ARIZONA			
Phoenix/Scottsdale			
(October 1-May 14)	106	38	144
(May 15-September 30)	72	38	110
Tucson			
(November 1-May 31)	85	34	119
(June 1-October 31)	67	34	101
ARKANSAS			
Little Rock	61	30	91
CALIFORNIA			
Los Angeles	109	42	151
Oakland	111	34	145
Sacramento	81	38	119
San Francisco	120	42	162

Table B-1 **Sampling of Per Diem Rates in the United States (Aug. 1998) in Dollars *(continued)***

Location	Lodging	Food	Total
COLORADO			
Boulder			
(May 1–October 31)	92	38	130
(November 1–April 30)	70	38	108
Colorado Springs			
(April 1–October 31)	76	30	106
(November 1–March 31)	63	30	93
Denver	92	34	126
CONNECTICUT			
Bridgeport/Danbury	96	38	134
Hartford	91	30	121
DELAWARE			
Wilmington	93	38	131
DISTRICT OF COLUMBIA	126	42	168
FLORIDA			
Daytona Beach			
(February 1–August 31)	90	34	124
(September 1–January 31)	54	34	88
Fort Lauderdale			
(December 15–April 30)	104	34	138
(May 1–December 14)	72	34	106
Jacksonville	73	30	103
Orlando	77	34	111
Tampa/St. Petersburg			
(January 1–April 30)	103	38	141
(May 1–December 31)	81	38	119
GEORGIA			
Atlanta	97	38	135
Columbus	63	30	93

Table B-1 **Sampling of Per Diem Rates in the United States (Aug. 1998) in Dollars** *(continued)*

Location	Lodging	Food	Total
IDAHO			
Boise	68	34	102
ILLINOIS			
Chicago	120	42	162
INDIANA			
Fort Wayne	52	30	82
Indianapolis	79	38	117
Lafayette	54	34	88
Nashville			
(June 1-October 31)	117	30	147
(November 1-May 31)	65	30	95
IOWA			
Des Moines	68	30	98
KANSAS			
Kansas City	88	42	130
KENTUCKY			
Louisville	71	38	109
LOUISIANA			
New Orleans	88	42	130
MAINE			
Portland			
(July 1-October 31)	86	38	124
(November 1-June 30)	63	38	101
Rockport			
(June 15-October 31)	102	34	136
(November 1-June 14)	58	34	92

Table B-1   **Sampling of Per Diem Rates in the United States (Aug. 1998) in Dollars** *(continued)*

Location	Lodging	Food	Total
MARYLAND			
Baltimore	110	38	148
St. Michaels			
(April 1-November 30)	130	38	168
(December 1-March 31)	103	38	141
MASSACHUSETTS			
Boston	116	42	158
Springfield	67	30	97
MICHIGAN			
Detroit	89	38	127
Midland	58	30	88
Pontiac/Troy	93	38	131
MINNESOTA			
Duluth			
(June 1-September 30)	66	38	104
(October 1-May 31)	57	38	95
Rochester	68	30	98
MISSISSIPPI			
Jackson	65	34	99
MISSOURI			
Kansas City	88	42	130
St. Louis	75	42	117
MONTANA			
Great Falls	52	30	82
NEBRASKA			
Lincoln	51	30	81
Omaha	67	34	101

Table B-1 **Sampling of Per Diem Rates in the United States (Aug. 1998) in Dollars** *(continued)*

Location	Lodging	Food	Total
NEVADA			
Las Vegas	80	38	118
Reno	57	34	91
NEW HAMPSHIRE			
Concord			
(June 1-October 31)	68	30	98
(November 1-May 31)	50	30	80
Durham			
(May 1-October 31)	71	30	101
(November 1-April 30)	63	30	93
Manchester	73	30	103
NEW JERSEY			
Atlantic City	84	38	122
Newark	94	42	136
NEW MEXICO			
Albuquerque	70	34	104
Santa Fe			
(May 1-October 31)	122	42	164
(November 1-April 30)	83	42	125
NEW YORK			
Albany	68	38	106
Buffalo	78	38	116
New York City	198	42	240
Rochester	65	42	107
NORTH CAROLINA			
Charlotte	71	38	109
OHIO			
Akron	72	34	106

Table B-1 **Sampling of Per Diem Rates in the United States (Aug. 1998) in Dollars** *(continued)*

Location	Lodging	Food	Total
OHIO *(continued)*			
Cleveland	83	38	121
Columbus	81	34	115
OKLAHOMA			
Oklahoma City	65	30	95
OREGON			
Portland	89	38	127
PENNSYLVANIA			
Chester/Radnor	99	42	141
Philadelphia	113	38	151
Pittsburgh	90	38	128
RHODE ISLAND			
Newport/Block Island			
(May 1-October 14)	111	42	153
(October 15-April 30)	81	42	123
SOUTH CAROLINA			
Charleston	100	34	134
SOUTH DAKOTA			
Rapid City			
(June 1-August 31)	84	30	114
(September 1-May 31)	50	30	80
Sioux Falls	56	30	86
TENNESSEE			
Memphis	79	30	109
Nashville	91	38	129
TEXAS			
Austin	85	34	119
Houston	79	38	117

Table B-1 **Sampling of Per Diem Rates in the United States (Aug. 1998) in Dollars** *(continued)*

Location	Lodging	Food	Total
UTAH			
Salt Lake City/Ogden	83	38	121
VERMONT			
Manchester	75	34	109
VIRGINIA			
Charlottesville	55	42	97
Richmond	77	38	115
Williamsburg			
(April 1–October 31)	99	34	133
(November 1–March 31)	59	34	93
WASHINGTON			
Bellingham	54	34	88
Seattle	116	38	154
Spokane	74	38	112
WEST VIRGINIA			
Berkeley Springs	89	30	119
Charleston	52	30	82
WISCONSIN			
Brookfield	74	38	112
Milwaukee	77	34	111
WYOMING			
Jackson			
(June 1–October 14)	105	42	147
(October 15–May 31)	76	42	118

International Per Diem Rates

The following are selected International Per Diem Rates obtained from the federal government Web site (**policyworks.gov/org/main/mt/**).

Rates vary by country, city, and time of year. You should ensure that you have current values before entering into any contract (see Table B-2).

Table B-2. **Sampling of International Per Diem Rates (Aug/1998) in Dollars**

Location	Lodging	Food	Total
AFGHANISTAN			
Kabul	102	100	202
Other	51	50	101
ARGENTINA			
Buenos Aires	235	87	322
AUSTRALIA			
Adelaide	109	70	179
Brisbane	101	67	168
Canberra	83	63	146
Darwin Northern Territory			
(October 1–March 31)	95	61	156
(April 1–September 30)	124	63	187
Melbourne	105	67	172
Perth	95	79	174
Sydney	111	81	192
AUSTRIA			
Innsbruck	97	79	176
Vienna	95	80	175
BAHAMAS, THE			
Grand Bahama Island			
(April 16 - 12/14)	121	78	199
(12/15 - April 15)	162	82	244
Other	129	85	214

Table B-2. Sampling of International Per Diem Rates (Aug/1998) in Dollars *(continued)*

Location	Lodging	Food	Total
BARBADOS			
Barbados			
(April 16–December 14)	97	97	194
(December 15–April 15)	155	102	257
BELGIUM			
Antwerp	105	72	177
Brussels	129	97	226
Florennes	61	39	100
BRAZIL			
Brasilia	189	86	275
Porto Alegre	99	87	186
Rio de Janeiro	117	78	195
BULGARIA			
Sofia	159	54	213
CAMBODIA			
Phnom Penh	136	50	186
CAMEROON			
Douala	86	56	142
Yaounde	118	70	188
CANADA			
Calgary (Alta)	65	48	113
Ottawa (Ont)	98	51	149
Quebec (Que)			
(October 1–April 30)	92	78	170
(May 1–September 30)	124	82	206
Toronto (Ont)	126	58	184
Vancouver (BC)			
(October 16–April 30)	116	79	195
(May 1–October 15)	169	84	253

Table B-2. Sampling of International Per Diem Rates (Aug/1998) in Dollars *(continued)*

Location	Lodging	Food	Total
CHILE			
Santiago	127	97	224
CHINA			
Beijing	129	78	207
Shanghai	138	88	226
COSTA RICA			
San Jose	84	50	134
CZECH REPUBLIC			
Prague	155	77	232
DENMARK			
Copenhagen	112	81	193
EGYPT			
Cairo	103	73	176
FINLAND			
Helsinki	107	85	192
FRANCE			
Paris	159	101	260
GERMANY			
Boeblingen	101	61	162
Duesseldorf	188	91	279
GREECE			
Athens	81	68	149
HONG KONG			
Hong Kong	221	122	343
HUNGARY			
Budapest	116	81	197

Table B-2. Sampling of International Per Diem Rates (Aug/1998) in Dollars *(continued)*

Location	Lodging	Food	Total
INDIA			
Calcutta	187	79	266
New Delhi	215	74	289
INDONESIA			
Bali	140	77	217
Jakarta	127	56	183
IRAN			
Tehran	97	58	155
IRAQ			
Baghdad	100	20	120
IRELAND			
Dublin	123	81	204
Limerick	107	68	175
ISRAEL			
Tel Aviv	179	91	270
ITALY			
Bologna	113	99	212
Milan	154	97	251
Rome	126	82	208
Venice	146	126	272
JAMAICA			
Kingston	133	87	220
JAPAN			
Nagasaki	105	91	196
Tokyo City	137	79	216
Yokohama	163	109	272

Table B-2. Sampling of International Per Diem Rates (Aug/1998) in Dollars *(continued)*

Location	Lodging	Food	Total
KOREA			
Seoul	121	91	212
KOREA, DEM. PEOPLE'S REP. OF			
Pyongyang	170	34	204
KUWAIT			
Kuwait City	231	106	337
LUXEMBOURG			
Luxembourg	123	83	206
MALAYSIA			
Kuala Lumpur	55	46	101
MEXICO			
Acapulco			
(April 15-December 15)	70	52	122
(December 16-April 14)	86	54	140
Mexico City, D.F.	171	94	265
MOROCCO			
Rabat	105	65	170
Tangier			
(October 1-May 31)	83	48	131
(June 1-September 30)	92	48	140
NETHERLANDS			
Amsterdam	116	81	197
Hague, The	101	68	169
Schiphol	116	81	197
NEW ZEALAND			
Auckland	105	67	172
Wellington	113	66	179

Table B-2. Sampling of International Per Diem Rates (Aug/1998) in Dollars *(continued)*

Location	Lodging	Food	Total
NORWAY			
Oslo	133	87	220
PANAMA			
Panama City	108	59	167
PHILIPPINES			
Manila	143	55	198
POLAND			
Warsaw	150	88	238
PORTUGAL			
Lisbon	143	85	228
RUSSIA			
Moscow	188	100	288
Saint Petersburg	195	124	319
SAUDI ARABIA			
Jeddah	81	77	158
Riyadh	103	93	196
SINGAPORE			
Singapore	117	72	189
SOUTH AFRICA			
Cape Town			
(May 1–September 30)	98	47	145
(October 1–April 30)	132	51	183
Johannesburg	73	43	116
Pretoria	98	46	144
SPAIN			
Madrid	146	88	234

Table B-2. Sampling of International Per Diem Rates (Aug/1998) in Dollars *(continued)*

Location	Lodging	Food	Total
SWEDEN			
Stockholm	120	101	221
SWITZERLAND			
Baden	126	74	200
Zurich	133	95	228
SYRIA			
Damascus	208	98	306
TAIWAN			
Taipei	96	77	173
THAILAND			
Bangkok	125	65	190
TURKEY			
Ankara	100	76	176
UNITED ARAB EMIRATES			
Abu Dhabi	121	88	209
Dubai	124	104	228
UNITED KINGDOM			
Bristol	130	64	194
Edinburgh	209	103	312
Liverpool	149	81	230
London	210	105	315
Manchester	190	93	283
Rochester	152	111	263
VENEZUELA			
Caracas	138	77	215

Glossary

The following is a list of key terms and phrases that are commonly used in the SAP industry. SAP changes its terminology about as often as it releases new versions of its software, so refer to the SAP Web site for updated terminology.

ABAP Development Workbench. The integrated development work environment for SAP. It includes the ABAP editor, screen painter, data dictionary, function builder, and menu painter.

ABAP Repository. All development objects are held within the repository. They can be viewed through transaction SE80.

Accelerated SAP (ASAP) Implementation. ASAP is an overall program for implementing SAP with an emphasis on reducing the time and effort required to install SAP R/3.

Advanced Planner and Optimizer (APO). Advanced Planner and Optimizer, which is used in supply chain management. Performs demand planning, scheduling, production planning, and communication of details to all levels of the supply chain.

Application Link Enabling (ALE). Application Link Enabling is used to maintain a distributed yet integrated R/3 envirnonment. This is done by both synchronous and asynchronous communication between different R/3 installations (ie. Vendor master records do not have to be all on the same system, but can be on several systems, and all systems can access all records).

Archive Developers Kit (ADK). A tool kit containing the code, documentation, and examples for developing the archive elements needed for the archiving transaction SARA.

Applications Server. The hardware that runs the software that interacts with the user's workstation, background programs, and print spooling, and that handles the communication to the database server. A typical SAP installation has several "App" servers per SAP environment.

Available to Promise (ATP). The time required to deliver a product. This can include factors such as manufacturing, delivery, resource allocation, and supply constraints.

Backflush. Posting of goods issued after their physical issue.

Bill of Material (BOM). A structure list of components that make up an assembly. BOMs can be for materials, equipment, documents, etc.

Business Application Program Interface (BAPI). A method of an SAP business object. You can think of it as a way to remotely call integrated functions from SAP (e.g., "create sales order" or "list purchase orders").

Batch Data Communication (BDC) Session. A programmatic method of entering data to the SAP system. Data for each screen of each transaction is put into a special format by a program and then is processed.

Build to Stock. The process whereby products are made and stocked before they are ordered by a customer.

Business Object Repository (BOR). Tied to BAPIs, the BOR is a collection of SAP Business Object types and their methods (see *SAP Business Objects*).

Business Warehouse (BW) or Business Information Warehouse (BIW). SAP's data warehouse, which can be used to aggregate and evaluate information from numerous sources. Users can run predefined reports or make up ad hoc queries.

Change Number. Shorthand for Engineering Change Number. It refers to an object in SAP that allows you to change several objects together at the same time and handle them all as one unit.

Characteristic. Part of the classification system, it is used to define a property of an object such as color.

Check Table. A table used to determine whether a value is allowed or not.

Class. Part of the classification system, it is used to group like objects (objects that have similar characteristics).

Class Hierarchy. A way of grouping classes within classes. For example, you can have one class of computers with subordinate classes of laptop, desktop, and server.

Client. The highest level of data separation in an R/3 environment.

Command Field. The little rectangular box at the top left-hand corner of the SAP GUI. Can be used to enter transaction codes (e.g., /NVA01).

Condition. A method of determining prices, taxes, and output. Usually driven by user criteria.

Configurable Material. Material that can have varying components based on a set of user-defined rules (called dependencies and constraints).

Cross Application Time Sheeet (CATS). An add-on application to SAP that allows the recording of actual times of individual employees. It is integrated across multiple areas including Controlling, Human Resources and MM-Serv.

Customizing. The act of configuring SAP to meet your exact company requirements.

Data Dictionary. The place in SAP where information is kept on how data is stored and displayed. This includes tables, domains, structures, matchcodes, and lock objects.

Database Server. The hardware that communicates directly between the database (such as Oracle or Informix) and the application server.

Dialog Programming. Programming transactions using the screen painter. Don't confuse this with interactive reporting, which is done through a simple ABAP report.

Distribution Channel. The channel through which customers can purchase materials or services. Typical distribution channels include direct, mail order, and wholesale.

Electronic Data Interchange (EDI). The movement of data between two systems.

Employee Self Service (ESS). An SAP R/3 Application that allows employees to access and maintain certain elements of their Human Resource (HR) data in the HR Management System. Examples of data include time sheet entry, address changes, and payroll deductions. Includes interfaces to Workflow and the Intranet.

Engineer to Order. One-of-a-kind products that are designed and made specifically for one customer.

Factory Calendar. The place in SAP where the working days are defined; for example, it is used in the determination of availability of materials.

Function Library. A collection of prebuilt subroutines (called functions).

Implementation Guide (IMG). A step-by-step tool that is organized by business function, which assists in showing all of the various customizations that are allowed within SAP.

Info Record. An info record is a record of the Logistics Information System (LIS). The LIS system acquires historical data for a variety of purposes, including reporting and data warehousing.

Internet Transaction Server (ITS). The hardware that resides between the Internet application and SAP. In simple terms, when an SAP link is requested on an Internet browser, the Internet Transaction Server establishes the connection to SAP, opens the dialog task, and builds up the HTML to be displayed back to the user.

Intermediate Document (IDoc). A set of predefined record layouts that represent a business transaction (such as a purchase or sales order). They are typically used to transfer data from one system to another.

Make-to-Order Production. Each product is made specifically to meet the customer-driven specifications. The product is not stocked.

Material Type. A field on the material master that is used to group materials together. It controls functions in screens, inventory, and accounting. Some of the standard SAP material types are:

DIEN—Service

FERT—Finished Product

HALB—Semi-Finished Product

HAWA—Trading Goods

KMAT—Configurable Material

ROH—Raw Material

VERP—Packaging

Master Schedule Planning (MSP). The planning of parts that are critical to operation, profits, or resources within a company.

Master Recipe. The list of tasks required to make a product.

Matchcode. A way to find records by information about the record (e.g., enter customer name to find the account numbers).

Material Requirement Planning (MRP). The process of trying to determine the procurement requirements of materials based on current stock levels, orders, future requirements, and other requirements.

Menu Painter. Used to define pull-down menus, function keys, and push buttons. It is used in conjunction with the screen painter.

Modules. SAP is comprised of several different modules. The acronyms for these modules are:

AM—Asset Management

CO—Controlling

FI—Finance

HR—Human Resources

MM—Material Management

PM—Plant Maintenance

PP—Production Planning

PS—Project System

QM—Quality Management

SD—Sales and Distribution

WM—Warehouse Management

WF—Workflow

Online Service System. SAP's site where you can enter problems and have SAP personnel review them. You can also browse through previous problems to see if a solution already exists for your problem.

POS System. Point of Sale systems are integrated equipment for the purpose of entering and collecting sales data.

Presentation Server. The computer that is used with the SAP GUI to run transactions. A presentation server can be a UNIX workstation or PC running Windows or the NT operating system.

Purchasing Area. Purchasing areas are part of a purchasing organization. The main use of the purchasing area is for reporting.

Purchasing Organization. An organizational level within the corporate hierarchy that can purchase products or services.

Quant. The quantity of a product within a storage bin.

Release Notes. Document outlining major changes between two versions of SAP.

Remote Function Call (RFC). A call to a function on a different system. RFCs are used extensively with BAPIs and can be used to perform business functions such as the creation of Sales Orders or the retrieval of basic information on a material master record.

SAP Business Object. An SAP Business Object can be anything from a product that a company sells to an employee or business process. The object is comprised of four layers:

Core Layer. Database tables containing the information about the object

Integrity Layer. Business rules relating to the object

Interface Layer. Defines the objects interface to the outside world

Access Layer. Defines the technologies that can access the object (i.e., RFCs)

SAP Office. Integrated office functions within SAP used primarily for communication.

SAPscript. SAP's word processing system.

Sales Area. A unique combination of sales organization, distribution channel, and division.

Sales Organization. An organizational level within the corporate hierarchy that can sell and distribute products or services.

Security Profile. A collection of authorizations for a user's logon. These authorizations limit access to various areas within SAP or control the way the transactions behave for the user. Sometimes referred to as an authorization profile.

Service. Services are generally nonstorable and nontransportable. Examples of Services are legal or repair services.

Session. When you log on to the SAP system, you create a session in which you can perform a transaction. If you open another SAP window, you have opened another session.

Screen Painter. A tool used to create screens and the flow logic behind them.

SCOPE. Supply Chain Optimization, Planning, and Execution. In general, SCOPE can be divided into these areas:

SAP APO (SAP Advanced Planner and Optimizer)

SAP BBP (SAP Business-to-Business Procurement)

SAP Logistics Execution System (SAP LES)

Spool Request. A spool request is created whenever information is sent to an output device in SAP (e.g., a printer). It contains details about the request along with a copy of the information sent.

Storage Bin. The finest granularity of inventory management in a warehouse.

Transport. The movement of development objects (reports, tables, screens, customizations, etc.) from one system to another.

Transport Requests. Transport requests are the containers for the objects that need to be transported from one system to another. The transport request also contains information about how the transport is to be done.

Valuation Area. Where material stocks are valued for accounting purposes. Can be either at the company or plant level.

Variant Configuration. A product that can be made up in a large number of combinations (such as a car or a computer). The product has a Bill of Material which, through the use of a classification system and routings, can be used to determine the lower level materials and assembly instructions of the product.

Work Breakdown Structure (WBS). Work breakdown structures are used in the project system to represent projects and the hierarchy of actions to be done within the project.

Workbench Organizer. The tool that records changes to all SAP objects, including programs, screens, data dictionary, and documentation. The Workbench Organizer can help coordinate software development.

Workflow (WF). A predefined sequence of steps that are performed to accomplish a business task. SAP's Workflow manager then manages these steps.

Index

NOTES

NOTES

NOTES

NOTES

NOTES

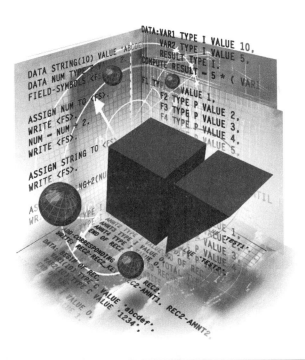

FREE SUBSCRIPTION FORM

To receive a FREE *SAP Technical Journal*, complete and return this form.

Name_____

Title_____

Company_____

Address_____

City_____ State/Province_____

Country_____ Zip/Postal Code_____

Telephone_____ Fax_____

E-mail Address_____

Please answer all questions, sign and date the card.

❑ YES! I wish to receive my FREE subscription to *SAP Technical Journal*.

❑ NO, I don't wish to subscribe

Signature (required)_____

Date (required)_____

1 What is your relationship to SAP? (check only one)
- 01 ❑ Customer
- 02 ❑ Third-Party vendor
- 03 ❑ Development partner
- 04 ❑ Consulting partner
- 05 ❑ Hardware partner
- 06 ❑ SAP Employee
- 07 ❑ Other_____

2 If a customer, is your R/3 System live?

Currently / Within the next 6 months
- 08 ❑ Yes   10 ❑ Yes
- 09 ❑ No   11 ❑ No

3 How many years have you been working with SAP products? (check only one)
- 12 ❑ Less than 1 year
- 13 ❑ 1 - 2 years
- 14 ❑ 2 - 5 years
- 15 ❑ Over five years

4 What is your current job function? (check only one)
- 16 ❑ Analyst/Program Analyst
- 17 ❑ Application Consultant
- 18 ❑ Application Developer
- 19 ❑ Basis Consultant
- 20 ❑ Basis Developer
- 21 ❑ Business Operations Manager
- 22 ❑ Design/Development or R&D Engineer
- 23 ❑ Network Engineer
- 24 ❑ Process Engineer
- 25 ❑ Product Manager
- 26 ❑ Quality/Reliability Manager
- 27 ❑ Software Engineer
- 28 ❑ Test Engineer
- 29 ❑ Web/Internet Professional
- 30 ❑ Other_____

5 Which SAP release(s) do you currently work with? (check ALL that apply)
- 31 ❑ R/2
- 32 ❑ R/3 3.x
- 32 ❑ R/3 2.x
- 34 ❑ R/3 4.x

6 Do you have Internet/intranet applications connected to SAP R/3?

Currently / Within the next 6 months
- 35 ❑ Yes   37 ❑ Yes
- 36 ❑ No   38 ❑ No

7 What SAP R/3 functionality do you use? (check all that apply)
- 39 ❑ Financial Accounting (FI)
- 40 ❑ Controlling (CO)
- 41 ❑ Asset Managment (AM)
- 42 ❑ Project System (PS)
- 43 ❑ Workflow (WF)
- 44 ❑ Industry Solutions (IS)
- 45 ❑ Human Resources (HR)
- 46 ❑ Plant Maintenance (PM)
- 47 ❑ Quality Management (QM)
- 48 ❑ Production Planning (PP)
- 49 ❑ Materials Management (MM)
- 50 ❑ Sales and Distribution (SD)

8 Which best describes your industry? (check only one)
- 51 ❑ Aerospace & Defense
- 52 ❑ Automotive
- 53 ❑ Banking/Insurance
- 54 ❑ Chemicals
- 55 ❑ Consumer Products
- 56 ❑ Consulting & Professional Services (please specify)_____
- 57 ❑ Computer Dealer (Reseller/Vendor)
- 58 ❑ Data Processing
- 59 ❑ Education
- 60 ❑ Entertainment/Tourism
- 61 ❑ Engineering & Construction
- 62 ❑ Healthcare
- 63 ❑ High Tech & Electronics
- 64 ❑ Media
- 65 ❑ Oil & Gas
- 66 ❑ Pharmaceuticals
- 67 ❑ Public Sector
- 68 ❑ Real Estate
- 69 ❑ Retail (not computers)
- 70 ❑ System House-Integrator or VAR/Systems/Integrators
- 71 ❑ Transportation
- 72 ❑ Telecommunications
- 73 ❑ Utilities
- 74 ❑ Other_____

9 What SAP R/3 infrastructure do you work with? (check ALL that apply)
- 75 ❑ OS/390   77 ❑ Windows NT
- 76 ❑ OS/400   78 ❑ UNIX

10 Which tools/languages do you use for SAP R/3 and SAP R/3-integrated solutions? (check ALL that apply)
- 79 ❑ ABAP
- 80 ❑ Active X
- 81 ❑ ALE
- 82 ❑ Batch
- 83 ❑ C/C ++
- 84 ❑ Cobol
- 85 ❑ COM/DCOM
- 86 ❑ CORBA
- 87 ❑ Delphi
- 88 ❑ DHTML
- 89 ❑ EDI
- 90 ❑ HTML
- 91 ❑ Java
- 92 ❑ JavaScript
- 93 ❑ PERL
- 94 ❑ PowerBuilder
- 95 ❑ SQL
- 96 ❑ Visual Basic
- 97 ❑ Other_____
- 98 ❑ None of the Above

FAX TO:
1-615-377-0525 or
SUBSCRIBE ONLINE
www.saptechjournal.com

11 What tools/topics are you interested in? (check ALL that apply)

- 099 ❑ Archiving
- 100 ❑ Application development tools
- 101 ❑ Application Link Enabling
- 102 ❑ Enterprise Management
- 103 ❑ Information Management
- 104 ❑ Internet/intranet
- 105 ❑ Middleware
- 106 ❑ Modeling
- 107 ❑ Performance Management
- 108 ❑ Reporting
- 109 ❑ Systems Management
- 110 ❑ Testing
- 111 ❑ Workflow
- 112 ❑ Other_____

12 How many total employees does your company have?

- 113 ❑ Under 100
- 114 ❑ 100 to 249
- 115 ❑ 250 to 499
- 116 ❑ 500 to 999
- 117 ❑ 1,000 to 4,999
- 118 ❑ 5,000 to 9,999
- 119 ❑ 10,000 or more

13 What is your company's total sales volume?

- 120 ❑ Under $10 million
- 121 ❑ $10 - $50 million
- 122 ❑ $50 - $250 million
- 123 ❑ $250 - $500 million
- 124 ❑ $500 million - $1 billion
- 125 ❑ $1 billion - $5 billion
- 126 ❑ Over $5 billion

Publisher reserves the right to determine qualification for free subscriptions. Terms of publication are subject to change without notice. *SAP Technical Journal* is available at no charge to qualified persons within the U.S. and Canada.

PLEASE MAKE SURE YOU'VE:
- ☞ **Signed and dated the form**
- ☞ **Filled out the form completely**
- ☞ **Applied postage**
- ☞ **Folded form in half and taped closed (do not staple)**

FOLD HERE FOR MAILING

CIRCULATION DEPARTMENT
55 HAWTHORNE ST STE 600
SAN FRANCISCO CA 94105-3912

SAP
TECHNICAL JOURNAL

PLACE STAMP HERE